The Concise Guide to
WHISKY

Published in 2017
by Igloo Books Ltd
Cottage Farm
Sywell
NN6 0BJ
www.igloobooks.com

LEO002 0417
4 6 8 10 9 7 5 3
ISBN 978-178197-965-5

Written by Helen Jaeger

Printed and manufactured in China

Contents

A Brief Introduction to Whisky

The Global rise in demand for Whisky is good news for distilleries all over the world, especially in traditional territories such as Scotland, where whisky found its fame hundreds of years ago. Whisky is not just a tipple for gentlemen of the upper classes, but has in fact seen a rise among female drinkers and middle classes; many brands are inexpensive, and Western countries have shifted towards a 'drink less but better' attitude.

Whisky is a fine choice of liqueur, but it helps to understand a little about its heritage in order to enjoy whisky to the full. This guide is an essential introduction to whisky, detailing its rich history, the fascinating methods of production, and outlining famous whisky-making regions and their popular whiskies. Discover the best ways to drink whisky, and learn to distinguish different types, from single malt to blended whiskies. Whisky doesn't have to be intimidating, even the most amateur connoisseur can become a whisky expert and identify new flavours and favourites with this definitive guide.

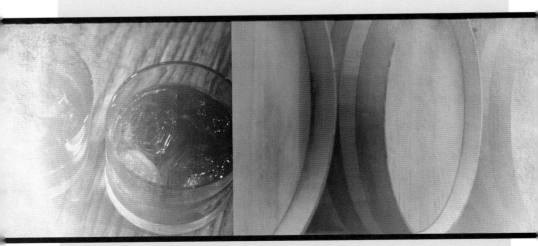

The Science

The science behind the making of whisky is actually fairly simple, but it is in fact very difficult to make it well. Scotland is probably the most famous whisky-producing country and is home to the highest number of distilleries, making world-famous single malts and blended whiskies. There are a number of countries that have successfully produced good quality whiskies, including Ireland, the USA, Canada and Japan, each distilling great variations of whisky which may differ in base product, alcohol content and quality.

Don't get bogged down with technical terminology; a basic knowledge of the production of whisky should aid your understanding of 'blends', 'malts' and 'grain'.

So, what is whisky?

Whisky is made from grains. These grains include barley, wheat, rye or corn and produce different varieties of whisky. To start with, sugar is extracted from the grains and fermented. Fermentation is a natural process that converts sugar to alcohol. The alcohol is then concentrated by the means of distillation, a technique used to separate mixtures which was founded centuries ago and ever since used in the production of whisky.

This mix is then referred to as the distillate, and must be aged in a wooden cask made of charred white oak, before it becomes whisky. There are laws in place which dictate the minimum amount of time that the whisky mixture must age within a cask, which is usually 2 – 3 years, dependant of the country of production. More often than not, distilleries age the whisky for a great number of additional years, perhaps 9 or 10, to develop a better taste.

Note:

Whisky is only aged within a cask; as soon as it is dispensed into the bottle it no longer ages, even if left in the bottle for a very long period of time. The cask itself actually contributes to the flavour of the whisky, so only in the cask does it technically age.

What is whisky made from?

Whisky is a type of alcoholic drink, made from fermented grain mash. Mash is created from crushed grain, stirred with boiling water. This creates a liquid, which is then collected and fermented.

Different grains are used for different varieties of whisky. These can include barley, malted barley, malted rye, wheat and corn. Whisky originated in Ireland and Scotland, but is now made all over the world.

'Whisky' v 'whiskey': which one is right?

The difference between 'whisky' and 'whiskey' is from provenance and geography. Whisky is the preferred spelling for Scotch whisky and Scotch-inspired drinks (and nowadays Canadian and Japanese whiskies), whereas 'whiskey' (with an 'e') refers to Irish and American roots. The word is of Celtic origin.

What does the word 'whisky' mean?

Whisky comes from the Gaelic word, 'uisceluisde', which means water. Distilled alcohol was known in Latin as 'aquae vitae' – water of life. This was translated in Irish Gaelic as 'uisce beatha' and in Scottish Gaelie as 'uisege beathat', which means 'lively water' (also 'water of life'). Other recorded variants include – 'uskebeaghe' (1581), 'usquebaugh' (1610), 'usquebath' (1621) and 'usquebae' (1715).

Early uses of whisky: as medicine

One of the first uses of whisky was as a medicine. It was used in medieval monasteries for the treatment of colic and smallpox. It was then used more widely. There are accounts of it being used by the Guild of Barbers and Surgeons. In medieval times, barbers helped monks, as monks were prohibited from shedding blood. Therefore, barbers took on the surgical procedures, such as lancing, bloodletting, leeching and tooth extraction. Whisky may well have helped with all of those!

World's first whisky distillery

Bushmills Distillery in County Antrim (Northern Ireland) is the oldest whisky distillery in the world, with a license dating back to 1609.

Whisky and royalty

The Irish *Annals Of Clonmacnoise* - a chronicle covering events in Ireland up to 1408 - include the death of an Irish chieftain from drinking too much 'aquae vaitae' (whisky) one Christmas. Another entry in 1494 in the Exchequer Rolls (an account of royal finances) details an order sent by the king to Friar John Cor for the production of around 500 bottles of whisky. James IV of Scotland (1488-1513) had a particular liking for whisky and in 1506 bought whisky from the Guild of Barbers and Surgeons, who then had a monopoly on whisky production. When Henry VII dissolved the monasteries (1536-1541), the King effectively ended monastic production of whisky. However the monks, part of the wider community, continued to make whisky and pass on their skills, as a way of sustaining themselves.

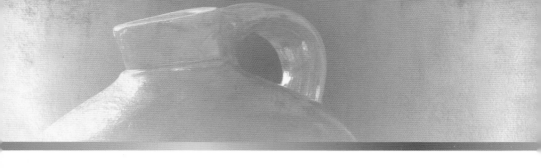

Whisky, taxes and the law: whisky goes underground

In 1707, the Act of Union between England and Scotland was passed. The price of whisky rose dramatically, as taxes on it increased. This led to illegal whisky making.

With the English Malt Tax of 1725, much of Scotland's whisky production went underground - illegal bottles were hidden under altars, in coffins, anywhere the inspectors would not be able to find them. Scottish distillers started making whisky at night, earning it the name 'moonshine.' (Making it at night kept the process hidden from inspectors). One hundred years later, distillation was legalised and 'moonshine' production ended.

Whisky in America

In America, whisky was used as currency during the American Revolution. When an extra tax was levied against it, the Whisky Rebellion broke out in 1791 under President George Washington. Violent clashes between farmers and state inspectors reached a climax with the death of tax inspector, General John Nashville. The whisky tax was eventually repealed under a different government. During the Prohibition Era (1920-1933), all alcohol sales were banned. In a nod to its past, whisky was exempt, if prescribed by a doctor or sold through pharmacies. Walgreen Pharmacy, a chain of pharmacies at the time, grew from around 20 stores to 400!

Contemporary whisky production

There are many types of whisky in production worldwide. Whisky is assessed according to its fermentation of grains, distillation process and length of ageing in wooden barrels – all affect flavour and quality. The four largest producers of whisky are America, Canada, Ireland and Scotland.

Road to whisky making: Timeline

200 BC	Babylonians practise distillery in Mesopotamia – but only for perfumes and aromatics.
3rd Century	Greeks have distillers at Alexandria – but not for alcohol.
9th Century	Arabs use distillation processes.
12th Century	Latin accounts have details on the distillation process.
13th Century	Italian records have information on distilling alcohol – the first time it's ever recorded.

Types of whisky

There are three types of whisky:

1. Malt whisky – made from malted barley

2. Grain whisky – made from maize or wheat

3. Blended whisky – a combination of malt and grain whisky

The Five Steps of Whisky Making

STEP 1

MILLING

Malted barley and grain are milled very fine. This enables the optimum conversion of starch to alcohol in the following four stages of whisky making production.

STEP 2

MASHING

Warm water is added to the milled, malted barley or grain. This is then mashed. During stage, starches are converted to fermentable sugars. The sugar liquid called 'wort' that runs during this process is used in the fermentation stage.

STEP 3

FERMENTATION

The wort is cooled into fermentation tanks. Then yeast of the Saccharomyces Cerevisiae species is added to the wort. This ferments for about 72 hours, during which the glucose converts into ethanol and carbon dioxide. This results in an alcoholic liquid of around 8-9% alcohol by volume, which is known as the 'wash.'

DISTILLATION

For malt whisky, the wash is pumped into copper pot stills, where it is heated to boil off the alcohol. Alcohol has a lower boiling temperature than water – at 78 degrees Celsius (as opposed to 100 degrees Celsius for water). The spirit driven off by heat from the wash is a vapour. This is condensed back into liquid (spirit) and distilled two, or even three times in copper pot stills. The first distillation produces a liquid known as 'low wines' and the second distillation creates the spirit. The second (and third) distillation is where the skills of a master distiller come to the fore.

For grain whisky, the wash is distilled in a continuous column still – also known as a Coffey or Patent still. This type of distillation produces a lightly flavoured spirit, which is broken down with de-mineralised water, before ageing.

AGEING

Ageing is the process whereby the spirit matures. It is the same for both malt and grain whisky. After distillation, the clear liquid (which can look like water) is put into oak casks and stored. The casks vary in size. During ageing the flavours of the spirit combine with the wood, which gives the whisky its eventual distinctive taste and appearance. Wood is porous so whisky will take on character from the wood around it. Most whiskies must be aged for a minimum of three years. Approximately 3% of whisky is lost each year to evaporation – this is known as the 'angel's share.'

Whisky Glossary

AGE STATEMENT
The age statement of a whisky is found on the label and refers to the youngest whisky in blended whisky products. Whiskies do not age while they are in the bottle.

ANGEL'S SHARE
The amount of whisky lost to evaporation while it is ageing in casks.

BARLEY
A common cereal from which a large range of whiskies are made.

BLENDING
The process of combining different whiskies to make a unique product.

BOURBON
A whisky made in America, it must contain a certain amount of cereal and is classified accordingly.

CASKS
Used for maturing spirit, casks have a direct influence on the flavour of the final product. Casks maybe used or new, charred or uncharred or may previously have held other spirits such as bourbon or sherry.

CASK STRENGTH
The strength at which the whisky comes out of the cask after ageing.

CHARRING
Exposing the inside of new barrels to flames to release flavours from the wood.

CHILL FILTRATION
Prevents hazing when bottles are stored at cold temperatures.

DISTILLATION
Process whereby spirit is separated from liquid using heat in the stills. The alcohol can be collected by condensation.

FERMENTATION
A slow process during which enzymes convert the glucose in malt and grain into ethanol and carbon dioxide.

GRAIN WHISKY
A whisky distilled by a continuous method either from wheat or maize and usually blended with malt whisky, but may also exist in its own right.

GRIST
The ground malt and grain used in mashing.

KILN
Area in which the malted barley is dried and infused with peat, usually at a commercial maltster's.

MALTING
The process of converting barley into malted barley by soaking it, which allows the barley to germinate.

MALT WHISKY
Malted barley mashed and fermented with yeast, before being distilled two or three time in a pot still and aged for a few years.

MATURATION
Also known as ageing. Spirit produced from distillation is placed in special casks and left to age, developing distinctive flavour and colour.

MARRYING
Several whiskies of similar ages are vatted together after initial maturation and allowed to mature together for a few more months.

NOSE
The aroma of a whisky.

PEAT
Substance made from compressed vegetable matter which is used in the malting process of barley. Peat adds flavour and subtlety.

PEATED MALT
Malted barley with strong smoky overtone.

POT STILLS
Vessels in which distillation takes place. Copper pot stills are used for malt whisky and Coffey or Patent stills for grain whisky.

PROOF
A system of defining alcohol strength. Linked to ABV – alcohol by volume, where this is the strength of a whisky is measured as a percentage in relation to the liquid as a whole.

SINGLE MALT
A malt whisky that has been made in a single distillery and not blended.

UISGE BEATHA
Gaelic for 'water of life', the original name of whisky.

VATTING
The mixing together of malt or grain whiskies from a distillery or different distilleries.

WASH
Wort after fermentation is an alcohol liquid referred to as the wash. The wash is the first stage of the fermentation process.

WASH STILL
The final pot still used in the distillation process.

WORT
Warm water is added to milled malted barley or grain and then mashed. At this stage, barley starches turn to sugar. The resulting sugary liquid is called wort and is used during the fermentation process.

YEAST
A living organism, which, when added to sugar produces alcohol and carbon dioxide through a process known as fermentation.

How to Taste

Whisky tasting involves all of your senses – sight, smell, taste and even touch. There are four key components of whisky evaluation:

1. Appearance

2. Smell

3. Taste

4. Finish

Appearance

When evaluating the appearance of a whisky, look at three main areas
– colour, viscosity and clarity. The colour of whisky can vary, from
completely clear like vodka to a deep treacle colour and many shades
of brown in between. The colour can indicate the type of cask used in
the ageing process and the length of maturation. The colour of whisky
is highly influenced by its contact with the surrounding wood in
which it is stored. As a basic rule, the longer the period of maturation,
the deeper and darker the colour of whisky. Many countries stipulate
three years as the minimum amount of time for whisky to be aged,
although many single malts are older than this. In addition, whisky
spirit is often matured in different types of casks – old sherry casks
yield a darker amber colour, while ex-bourbon casks are more of a
honey-yellow. To evaluate the colour of whisky, look at it against a
white background (e.g. a sheet of white paper) and tilt the glass away
from yourself for a really good look.

Viscosity is the measure of thickness of the liquid. Water has low
viscosity, whereas syrup has high viscosity. Viscosity can be an
indicator to the age of a whisky, as older whiskies tend to be 'thicker.'
To evaluate the viscosity, swirl the whisky in a glass, so that it whirls
towards the top of the glass. Then let it settle. Pay attention to long
tear-drop streaks down the inside of the glass (often referred to as
'legs'). Thicker, slow-moving legs indicate an older whisky; thin fast
moving legs indicate a younger whisky. Long legs indicate that the
whisky is high in alcohol.

Whisky may be chill-filtered to remove haziness or cloudiness, which
gives the whisky clarity. Some critics argue this removes oily, fatty
compounds, thus reducing the complexity of the drink. Non-chill-
filtered whiskies go cloudy when water is added to them and are said
to have a fuller flavour.

Smell

The nose can distinguish hundreds of different smells. To evaluate the smell of a whisky, swirl the whisky in the glass and place your nose at the top of the glass, so that you can take a small, short smell of the drink. Take your nose away from the glass after each evaluation. Try to associate a word with each aroma you detect – for example smoky like a log fire or spicy like cinnamon. Adding water to whisky can help you detect subtle aromas.

Taste

There are four common tastes – sweet, sour, salty and bitter. Japanese culture recognises a fifth – 'umami' meaning flavour or savouriness. To evaluate the taste of a whisky, take a small sip and move the liquid around in your mouth for a couple of seconds, before swallowing. Again, try to associate the taste with a flavour you know – for example, blueberries.

As you move the fluid around in your mouth, it is possible to get a sense of the feel of it in your mouth – this is literally known as 'mouthfeel.' Mouth-feel is the weight or thickness of the whisky in your mouth – it can vary from thin and light to thick and full.

Finish

The finish refers to the amount of time that the flavours of a whisky linger on your palate after swallowing. The length of the finish can be anything from short through medium to long. The best whiskies have a lingering finish – you can still taste them in your mouth after you have swallowed the liquid and, if it's a good whisky, you should be able to enjoy it for some time.

Whisky Evaluation

Here is a sample evaluation on a famous whisky,
The Macallan, by the Masters of Malt.

Nose:
*Rich, malty nose with hints of toffee apples, brandy snaps
and a hint of treacle. Rich notes of winter spice, pepper
and cooked fruit.*

Palate:
*Pear juice, hints of sweet Normandy cider and allspice.
Thick, biscuity malt, a little toasted barley and vanilla
ice cream.*

Finish:
*Dried apricot and creamy caramel. A touch of mixed
peels and spice.*

Overall:
*Full of malt and fruity flavour, typical of one of Speyside's
best-loved distilleries.*

As you read through this book, you may be interested to
find out more about individual whiskies and explore some
for yourself. Enjoy the world of whisky!

Whiskies From Around the World

Whisky is produced all over the world. Although Scotland is the leading producer of whisky, demand for this popular spirit has risen globally, sparking a growth in the number of countries producing whisky. Currently there are over 20 countries worldwide making and selling very famous whiskies.

Europe

Sweden
Scotland
Ireland
England
Wales
Holland
France
Switzerland

Canada

USA

Japan

India

South Africa

Australia

Tasmania

Finding your tipple

To the whisky novice, the sheer amount of whiskies available may seem intimidating. There are hundreds of brands from all over the world, of all ages, some of which can be expensive! There are plenty of affordable expressions out there too, and choosing one doesn't have to be daunting. The Ultimate Guide to Whisky explores the most famous whisky-producing countries in the world, offering an insight into their rich histories and their products, in order to help you begin your whisky tasting journey. From traditional, best-selling whiskies, to award-winning newcomers, the next sections of this book will cover some great whiskies for the beginner, and even the most seasoned whisky connoisseur.

Whisky pages

The following sections will cover whiskies from Scotland, Ireland, The USA, Canada, Japan, Europe and the rest of the world. Each page details a different distillery, providing a brief introduction into its history, alongside tasting notes for the distillery's whisky. Now that you know the basics in whisky tasting, you can use this book to learn more about specific brands and their heritages before trying them for yourself. Most of these popular whiskies make various expressions, so don't just stick to the whiskies outlined in this book. Explore older whiskies, younger whiskies, and train your palate to recognise flavour and mouthfeel. Whisky has a fascinating history, and each whisky has its own story to tell. Explore beyond the famous Scotch whiskies and discover a whole world of delicious blends and malts.

SCOTLAND

Scottish whiskies are some of the most popular and respected whiskies in the world. Some are heavy and flavoured with peat and others are light and fruity. Whiskies distilled by the sea often have a slightly saline taste. There are distinct regions of Scottish whisky production and whisky making has a long and rich tradition in Scotland, which continues to this day.

SCOTLAND

HISTORY

Scottish whisky is malt or grain whisky made in Scotland. It is frequently referred to simply as 'scotch'. Originally all Scottish whisky was made from malt. From the 1900s onwards, however, it also began to be made from wheat and rye.

The first written reference to Scottish whisky is in 1495. It is in the Exchequeur Rolls of Scotland, where a friar called John Cor was asked to provide whisky for the royal court. He was asked, 'by order of the king' to make eights bolls of malt (described as 'aquae vitae', the old Gaelic expression for whisky). The modern equivalent of eight bolls is about 1,500 bottles.

By 1644 whisky production in Scotland was so well established, that it began to be taxed. The move was not popular and many people started to produce illicit whisky. In 1780 there were eight recorded legal distilleries in Scotland – with around 400 illegal ones. This coined the term 'moonshine', since much illegal whisky was made at night. By 1823 Parliament had recognised the problem and changed the laws. Now it was harder for the illicit stills to operate, but restrictions on licensed ones were eased.

TYPES OF SCOTCH

There are five categories of Scottish whisky: single malt, single grain, blended malt, blended grain and blended Scotch whisky.

- A single malt is produced from malt made in one distillery. It is made from water and malted barley in pot stills.

- A single grain whisky is distilled at one distillery, but, as well as water and malted barley, it contains other grains.

- Blended malts comprise single malts from different distilleries that are blended in the bottle.

- Blended grains contain a blend of two more single grain whiskies from different distilleries.

- Blended Scottish whisky, on the other hand, is a blend of one or more single malts with one or more single grains.

LEGAL REGULATIONS

There are strict laws governing the production and labelling of Scottish whisky. By law, all Scottish whisky must be aged in oak barrels for at least three years. In any blended whisky, the youngest whisky must appear on the bottle. It must also be produced in a distillery in Scotland and be made from malted barley (to which other grains can be added) produced at the same distillery. The spirit must then be aged in Scotland and contain no added substances, such as caramel (for colour).

Scottish whisky must also be bottled and labelled in Scotland. Bottlers are not allowed to use a distillery name unless the whisky was made there. Labels can, however, indicate which region the whisky was made in – for example, Speyside or Islay.

The Scottish Whisky Association oversees whisky regulations and distilleries.

WHISKY REGIONS

Scotland is divided into five whisky-producing regions: Speyside, Highlands, Lowlands, Islay and Campbeltown.

Speyside is located around the Spey river valley in northeast Scotland, of which Strathspey is a part. Once part of the Highlands, it has half of all Scottish distilleries and so is now a region in its own right. The region includes such big-name brands as Cragganmore, Glenfiddich, Glenlivet and The Macallan, among others. Speyside whiskies are usually light and grassy or rich and sweet with a good balance.

The Highlands are divided into four sub-regions. Northern Highland whiskies are full, sweet and rich. Southern Highland whiskies are lighter, drier and fruitier. Eastern Highland whiskies are dry and fruity. Western Highland whiskies are peaty and smoky. The region includes Dalwhinnie (the highest Scottish distillery), Balblair and Glenmorangie, as well as the Islands, which are all the Scottish islands that have distilleries, except for Islay. These islands include Jura, Scapa and Talisker.

The Lowlands, located in the lowlands of Scotland, has just three distilleries currently working – Auchentoshan, Bladnoch and Glenkinchie – although there is possibility of new distilleries starting to produce whisky soon. Lowland whiskies are often light, gentle and dry, with hints of fruit and floral notes.

Campbeltown was once the 'Victorian capital of whisky production'. It is located by Campbeltown Loch on the Kintyre Peninsula. Now it has around 30 distilleries, including Glen Scotia and Springbank. Campbeltown whiskies are often dry and smoky and influenced by nearness to the coast.

Islay is the southern most island of the Inner Hebrides of Scotland. Its capital is Bowmore and it is the fifth largest Scottish island. One of its main commercial activities is whisky production and the island has eight whisky-producing distilleries, which include Bowmore, Lagavulin and Laphraoig. Islay whiskies are often peaty and salty.

SINGLE V BLENDED

Blended Scottish whisky is Scotland's best-selling spirit and accounts for around 90% of Scotland's whisky production. Famous blends include Bell's, The Famous Grouse, Grant's, Johnnie Walker, Teacher's and White Horse.

SPEYBURN

ABOUT

HISTORY

The Speyburn- Glenlivit Distillery was founded in 1897 by John Hopkins & Company. John Hopkins chose the location because of its unpolluted water supply. Hopkins appointed famous distillery architect, Charles C. Doig, to design his distillery.

TOWARDS SUCCESS

Speyburn includes a large range of whiskies. Bradan Orach, which is Gaelic for 'Golden Salmon', is matured in ex-bourbon casks. Bright amber in colour, it includes notes of apples, honey, lemon, vanilla and honey with a spicy finish. Speyburn 10 year old single malt has hints of toffee, butterscotch and lemon. Speyburn 25 year old single malt is matured for a quarter of a century in white oak sherry and bourbon casks. This slow process results in a light amber whisky with complexity and balance.

Speyburn Single Highland Scotch Malt whisky is a popular whisky exported throughout the world and is often cited as being in the top 10 best-seller single malt whiskies in the USA. Water is the secret treasure at the heart of the Speyburn single malt. This whisky uses water from the fast-flowing Granty Burn, a tributary of the river Spey, which is a salmon-fishing river famed for its purity.

Speyburn 10 Years Old

NOSE

Citrus, orange peel, lemon, herbs, woody and minty.

TASTE

Cereal, malt, aniseed and smoky.

APPEARANCE

Pale gold with amber.

GLENFIDDICH

SCOTLAND

ABOUT

A FAMILY AFFAIR

In the summer of 1886, a Scotsman named William Grant began to build a distillery by hand with the help of his seven sons and two daughters. After a single year of work, it was ready and the first whisky was produced on Christmas Day 1887. Grant named it 'Glenfiddich', Scottish for 'Valley of the deer'. Glenfiddich remains entirely family owned to this day.

Over a hundred years later Glenfiddich is the world's best-selling single malt, sold in 180 countries and accounting for about 35% of single malt sales.

TASTES OF DISTINCTION

The distillery uses water from the Robbie Dhu spring, which flows through peat and over granite. It boils juniper bushes in its stills to neutralise natural sulphur from barley and cleanse the copper until it is 'sweet'. The distillery has coppersmiths on site.

NOTABLE RELEASES

Glenfiddich is bottled at many ages, but notable releases include a 50 year old malt, produced from nine casks laid down in 1930 (nine for each of William Grant's children), a 64 year old malt, of which only 61 bottles were produced and the most expensive single malt ever auctioned, 'Janet Sheed Roberts', named after the last grandchild of Glenfiddich's founder.

Glenfiddich 15 Year Old

NOSE

Orange and citrus tones, pears, sherry and dry wood. Light hints of cinnamon and vanilla.

TASTE

Sweet, with fruits, raisins and spicy with an oaky finish.

APPEARANCE

Dark golden.

CRAGGANMORE

SCOTLAND

BIG MAN, BIG VISION

'Big' John Smith - said to have been the most experienced distiller of his day - founded Cragganmore Distillery in 1869. Smith had been manager of Glenlivet, Macallan and Wishaw distilleries. He persuaded his landlord to lease in Ballindalloch, Scotland. Smith chose the site for its proximity both to the waters of Craggan Burn and Strathspey Railway. Smith was a great railway enthusiast, even though he weighed 22 stone (140kg) and had to travel in the Guard's van.

CLOSING DOWN

The distillery closed in 1917, when the government restricted barley supply, reopening two years later, only for the railway station to burn down three years after that. Cragganmore closed again in the early 1930s recession, reopening in 1934. Wartime and a shortage of barley meant production was limited for five years.

Uniquely, Cragganmore has flat-topped spirit stills and uses wooden worm-tubs. In 1989 Cragganmore Distillers Edition won Gold Medal at the International Wine and Spirit competition.

Cragganmore 1998 Distiller's Edition

NOSE

Strawberries, sherry, apple peel, almonds and gingerbread.

TASTE

Spicy and fruity with strong berry overtones.

APPEARANCE

Golden yellow and clear.

ABOUT

FROM MEDIEVAL TIMES

The Macallan Distillery is a single malt Scotch whisky distillery in Craigellachie, Moray. In 1543 the Bishop of Moray gave the lands of Easter Ellochy, near the Spey River, to Duncan Grant. Grant built a house called Easter Elchie House. In 1824 a local famer, Alexander Reid, was granted one of the earliest licenses to distil whisky there. Almost two hundred years later, The Macallan Estate produces the world's third most popular single malt.

ATTENTION TO DETAIL

The Macallan uses a barley variety called Minstrel, rich and oily, grown exclusively for the Estate. The brand has collaborated with some of the world's top photographers, including Ian Rankin, Albert Watson and Annie Leibovitz. Each year it launches a limited edition whisky or range of whiskies in collaboration with a photographer.

A bottle of The Macallan 64-year-old single malt whisky in a Lalique crystal decanter has sold at auction for a record-breaking $460,000.

The Macallan Amber

NOSE

Light, floral, citrus with vanilla notes.

TASTE

Apples and lemons with a cinnamon twist.

APPEARANCE

Amber.

DALWHINNIE

ABOUT

LOCATION, LOCATION, LOCATION

For a number of years, Dalwhinnie prided itself on being the highest distillery in Scotland. The water it's made from comes from the most remote and wild mountain source of any malt. The source, Lochan an Doire-Uaine, (Gaelic for "lake in the green grove"), lies at 2,000 feet in the Drumochter Hills. The pure spring water used in distilling Dalwhinnie flows over peat through Allt an t'Sluic, the distillery burn. No other distillery may use water from this source. Its mountainous location is key to Dalwhinnie's character, which is described as peaty and heathery.

HISTORY

In 1897, John Grant, George Sellar and Alexander Mackenzie founded the Strathspey distillery. Production started in 1898, but the partnership went bankrupt the same year. The distillery was sold to AP Blyth in 1898 and renamed Dalwhinnie. Later, it became part of the very first US investment in the Scotch whisky industry.

Dalwhinnie 15 Year Old

NOSE

Floral, apple blossom, honey, toffee, fruit salad, custard and a hint of light smoke.

TASTE

Malty, walnuts, honey, vanilla with light spice.

APPEARANCE

Pale gold, like Chardonnay wine.

WHISKY AND THE LAW

Illicit distilleries were a fact of life in Scotland from medieval times up to the passing of the Excise Act in 1823. Under this new law, distilleries could apply for a license to make whisky. Alexander Gordon, fourth Duke of Gordon, was supportive of the legislation. One of his tenants, George Smith, who'd been operating an illegal distillery, successfully applied for a license and then opened the Glenlivet Distillery.

SUCCESS IN SCOTLAND
- AND BEYOND

In 1824 the first Glenlivet Distillery had been established in Upper Drumin. It was so successful, that a bigger site was created at Minmore just thirty years later. The distillery stayed open during the Great Depression – only closing during the Second World War by Government decision. After the war, whisky restrictions were lifted to encourage export. Glenlivet is now the bestselling malt whisky in the United States.

Glenlivet 12 Year Old

NOSE

Creamy vanilla, toffee, pastries, fudge, aniseed and oak.

TASTE

Aniseed, dried peels and fudge with a smooth buttery note.

APPEARANCE

Pale gold.

SCOTLAND

BALBLAIR

ABOUT

AGE AND PEDIGREE

Balblair is one of the oldest distilleries in Scotland, founded in 1790. Located in the Northern Highlands of Scotland, it was created by John Ross on the shores of Dornoch Firth in the village of Edderton. The village takes its name from the ancient settlement of Eadar Dun, which means 'between the forts'. The area was known as 'parish of the peats' – referring to an abundance of peat in the surrounding soil. The present distillery buildings date from the 1890s.

ORIGINAL IS BEST

Originally founded in 1790, the distillery was rebuilt in 1895 by the designer Charles C. Doig to be closer to Edderton Railway Station. However, the original water source was so good, that the rebuilt distillery chose to ignore a nearby burn in favour of the original Ault Dearg burn. Balblair still uses the slightly peaty water from Ault Dearg burn, which has to be tankered to the distillery.

Balblair 1989 Single Malt

NOSE

Spicy, banana, sultana and nutty.

TASTE

Toffee and spicy fruit with cocoa.

APPEARANCE

Orange-gold.

ARDMORE

SCOTLAND

ABOUT

BLENDED TO PERFECTION

Founded in 1898 by one of Scotland's most famous whisky families, Ardmore Distillery was established by Adam Teacher, son of whisky entrepreneur William Teacher. He wanted to ensure a good supply of whisky for Teacher's blended whisky, which was becoming increasingly popular. Limited amounts of the single malt were produced, including an exclusive 12 year old to mark the distillery's centenary in 1998. However, whisky fans like Ardmore and the distillery has produced a more widely-available single malt.

TRADITIONAL METHODS ONLY

Ardmore prefers to use traditional distilling methods. The distillery's original configuration was one coal-fired wash and one coal-fired spirit still - power provided by a coal-fired steam engine. By 1974 it had eight stills but, until early 2001, used coal to fire them. It uses the aromatic smoke from natural, Highland peat fires to dry malted barley. Its whisky is also double matured – a method popular in the 19th century but relatively expensive nowadays. The Still House can be seen today.

Ardmore Traditional Cask

NOSE

Caramel, oak and light peat.

TASTE

Barley, bourbon, smoky and peaty with a touch of vanilla.

APPEARANCE

Dark bronze.

GLENMORANGIE

ABOUT

HISTORY

Alcohol was first produced at Morangie Farm in Ross-shire in Scotland in 1738, when a brewery was built. Around a hundred years later ex-distillery manager, William Matheson, acquired the farm, converting the brewery to a whisky distillery.

In 1918 Macdonald and Muir bought the distillery. It survived Prohibition, the Great Depression and two world wars. The company protected its future by securing land around the Tarlogie Springs, its water source, in 1990 by buying 650 acres. Since 1983, Glenmorangie has been the top selling single malt whisky in Scotland. The distillery produces around 10 million bottles a year.

Glenmorangie owns its own woodland in the Ozark Mountains in Missouri, earmarking individual trees for casks. New casks are aired for two years, and then leased to Jack Daniel's and Heaven Hill to mature bourbon in for four years, before coming to Glenmorangie.

Glenmorangie 10 Year Old

NOSE

Apples, nectarines, lemons and fruit with a touch of spice.

TASTE

Vanilla, cream, toffee and tiramisu.

APPEARANCE

Bright yellowy-gold and pale.

LOCH LOMOND

SCOTLAND

HISTORY

Loch Lomond is a distillery in Alexandria, Scotland, close to Loch Lomond. The Bulloch family, with their own label whisky, gin and vodka, purchased Loch Lomond Distillery in 1985. Loch Lomond is the only distillery in Scotland that produces both grain whisky and malt whisky. It has an annual production of 10 million litres of grain alcohol and 2.5 million litres of malt alcohol - the equivalent of 43 million standard bottles of whisky. Their single malt and single grain whiskies are also used for making Loch Lomond blended whisky.

VERSATILITY

Most Scotch malt whisky distilleries, because of the design of the stills, produce only one type of spirit. However, Loch Lomond has four stills with rectifying heads and two conventional pot stills with traditional 'swan necks'. This allows them to produce different styles of whiskies.

Loch Lomond Single Malt

NOSE

Woody, leathery and musty.

TASTE

Hay, cereal, biscuits and a touch of mustiness.

APPEARANCE

Amber gold.

ANCNOC

HISTORY

In 1892 John Morrison bought the Knock estate. The discovery of several springs of pure water on the southern slopes of Knock Hill, combined with the fact that the surrounding land was full of peat and barley and the Great North Railway line ran nearby made it an obvious choice for making whisky. Knockdhu Distillery, as it was called at the time, opened in 1894. At that time, two pot stills were able to turn out 2,500 gallons of spirit per week – quite an achievement. The malt from Knockdhu Distillery was renamed AnCnoc in 1993 to avoid confusion with Knockando.

BLACK HILL WHISKY

Knockdhu Distillery is under 'Knock Hill', known to the local villagers by its Gaelic name of 'Cnoc Dubh', which provides the source of the pure clear spring water for the malt. At certain times of the year, the hill appears black with heather and other vegetation when seen from the distance. Knockdhu comes from the Gaelic Cnoc Dhubh meaning 'black hill'. A traditional cast iron mash tun is used in the mashing process along with washbacks made from Douglas fir.

AnCnoc 35 Year Old

NOSE

Fruits, apple and sultana, citrus and a hint of woodvines.

TASTE

Fruity, cinnamon with biscuity notes, cedar wood and peppery finish.

APPEARANCE

Bright gold and coppery.

GLENKINCHIE

HISTORY

The agricultural revolution of the late 18th Century brought barley to East Lothian, earning the area the name 'Garden of Scotland'. Barley was often grown on land manured with local seaweed. Glenkinchie lies in a valley of the Kinchie Burn about 15 miles from Edinburgh. It was founded in 1825 by brothers John and George Rate and originally called Milton Distillery.

Glenkinchie was rebuilt in the 1890s. It was one of the five original Lowland distillers to form Scottish Malt Distillers Ltd. and one of very few distilleries to continue production throughout the Second World War.

TRADTIONAL METHODS

Wooden washbacks are used for fermentation, made from Oregon Pine and Canadian Larch. Glenkinchie's copper pot stills are among the largest in the industry, producing 340,000 gallons annually.

Glenkinchie 12 Year Old

NOSE

Honey, cereal, barley and nutty.

TASTE

Stewed fruits, calvados, madeira and oaky tones.

APPEARANCE

Rich, pale gold.

AUCHENTOSHAN

SCOTLAND

ABOUT

HISTORY

Auchentoshan is found near Glasgow in the west of Scotland. In fact, it's known as 'Glasgow's malt whisky'. Auchentoshan was granted its licence in 1823. During the Second World War, bombing on the Clydebank Shipyards, which lie nearby, left the distillery damaged with a large loss of spirit. In 1948, reconstruction began and the distillery was given the new name 'Auchentoshan'. It had originally been known as 'Duntocher'. Geographically, the distillery lies only just within the Lowlands, however, Auchentoshan's water source – near the Cochna Loch in the Kilpatrick Hills – is in the Highlands.

TRIPLE DISTILLATION

Auchentoshan is one of few triple-distilled single malts in Scotland.

Generally the final stage of Scotch whisky production involves distilling the fermented mash in two copper stills. In Auchentoshan, a third still, known as the 'intermediate still', helps to give a final spirit strength of 81% ABV (162 proof). This triple distillation, in addition to an unpeated malt, gives Auchentoshan a more delicate and sweet flavour than other scotch whiskies.

Auchentoshan 12 Year Old

NOSE

Cereal and fruits.

TASTE

Barley, vanilla and tannins.

APPEARANCE

Deep amber.

ABOUT

HISTORY

Bladnoch Distillery is the most southerly distillery in Scotland and is on the banks of the River Bladnoch.

The distillery was established in 1817 by the brothers McClelland: John and Thomas, who licensed it in 1825. Part of a farm, Bladnoch used barley from surrounding fields. By 1845 twenty workers were employed, converting 16,000 bushels of barley a year into whisky. In the twentieth century it went through a series of closures and ownership changes, but currently is one of six Lowland distilleries.

NORTHERN IRISH CONNECTIONS

Built in 1817, the distillery was sold in 1911 to the Belfast based whisky merchant Dunville & Co., who were in need of stocks of Scotch whisky to fulfil customer demand. After being sold to Arthur Bell in 1983, Bladnoch was then sold to another Northern Irishman, Raymond Armstrong. Armstrong had intended to convert the distillery into a guesthouse, but changed his mind, so that whisky production recommenced at the distillery.

Bladnoch 10 Year Old

NOSE

Fruity, caramel, corn and linseed oil.

TASTE

Dry, biscuits, oaky and mixed peel.

APPEARANCE

Pale straw.

SPRINGBANK

ABOUT

HISTORY

Springbank is located at the edge of Cambeltown Loch on the Kintyre Peninsula in Western Scotland. At one time Cambeltown boasted 34 working distilleries, despite having only 5,000 inhabitants, and proclaimed itself 'whisky capital of the world'. The Mitchell clan founded Springbank in 1828.

Springbank is one of the most traditional distilleries in Scotland. All stages of production - from the malting of the barley through to the bottling of the finished whisky - are carried out by hand on site. Only two distilleries in Scotland do the complete process. The malt itself is distilled two and a half times, with the result that some of the spirit has been distilled twice and some three times.

FAMILY OWNED

Springbank is one of a few remaining family -owned distilleries with 184 years of experience as a whisky producer. Nearly all of its whisky is sold as a single malt and very little appears in blends. Springbank only produces two of its own blends for consumption.

Springbank 10 Year Old

NOSE

Oaky, peaty, earthy, fruity and salty.

TASTE

Cereals, sweet, peaty, nutty and smoky.

APPEARANCE

Light and golden.

GLEN SCOTIA

ABOUT

HISTORY

Glen Scotia opened in 1832, known simply as 'Scotia' when it was first founded by Steward & Galbraith and Company, who ran the distillery for almost 60 years. Prohibition, bankruptcy and two world wars had a negative effect on Glen Scotia. Nowadays the distillery operates with just three employees, making it one of the smallest whisky distilleries in Scotland. But it is very efficient – with annual production at around 150,000. It's one of three Cambeltown distilleries and the only one producing single malt.

HAUNTED

Industrialist Duncan Cambell bought the distillery in 1891 and constructed malting floors, which run horizontally across Campbeltown's main street. Unfortunately, Cambell committed suicide, after realising he'd been tricked out of a fortune in a business deal. He drowned himself in Campbeltown Loch – the very loch that was created to serve as the water source for whisky making. It's said his ghost still haunts the distillery.

Glen Scotia 12 Year Old

NOSE

Oily, touch of tar, charcoal and quite pungent.

TASTE

Peaty, sweet, fruity and woody.

APPEARANCE

Dark caramel.

LAPHROAIG

HISTORY

Laphraoig is an Islay single malt distillery. It's situated on the head of Loch Laphraoig on the south coast of the Isle of Islay. Donald and Alexander Johnston, two brothers from the Clan Donald, founded the distillery in 1825.

During American prohibition, the distillery successfully convinced the American market the drink was not really whisky and could be sold under the label 'medicinal spirit.'

ROYAL FAVOUR

Laphroaig has been the only whisky to carry the Royal Warrant of the Prince of Wales, who awarded the honour in person during a visit in 1994. It's apparently his favourite tipple.

FOR PEAT'S SAKE

Laphraoig is one of the strongest flavoured Scotch whiskies with a heavy peaty taste. Laphraoig uses quarter casks – a smaller cask which was favoured in the 1700s, as mules could carry them more easily. This means the contact between wood and spirit is greater, too.

In 1994, the distillery created the 'Friends of Laphroaig'. Friends are granted a lifetime lease of one square foot of land on Islay.

Laphroaig 10 Year Old

 NOSE

Peaty, spicy, liquorice notes and salty.

TASTE

Vanilla, seaweed, oak hints and spices.

APPEARANCE

Sparkling gold.

BOWMORE

ABOUT

ENTREPRENEURS AND CONSULS

Bowmore is a whisky distillery in the capital of the isle of Islay, part of the Inner Hebrides. It lies on the shores of Loch Indaal and is said to be one of the oldest distilleries in Scotland, going back to 1779. John P Simpson, a local entrepreneur, was its original founder. Simpson sold the distillery to the Mutter family. James Mutter commissioned the building of a steam ship especially to carry barley from mainland Scotland and whisky to Glasgow. Mutter sold the distillery in 1925.

During the Second World War, whisky production was halted. Instead, the distillery was the base of RAF Coastal Command, who operated flying boats from the loch on attacks on enemy U-boats.

Two million litres of whisky are made annually with production methods that have hardly changed over the centuries.

SOCIAL CONCERN

Bowmore prides itself on its social concern. Waste heat from the distillation process heats a nearby public swimming pool, which was built in a former warehouse.

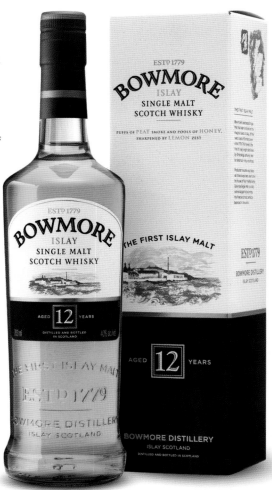

Bowmore 12 Year Old

NOSE

Peaty, smoky, heathers, ash, orange and floral.

TASTE

Peaty, smoky, blossoms, oily with some sweetness.

APPEARANCE

Amber gold.

LAGAVULIN

STABLE OF THE WHITE HORSE

Lagavulin is situated on a small bay near the south coast on the island of Islay. It stands near the ruins of Dunyvaig Castle, once the stronghold of the Lords of Isles. In 1816 local famer John Johnston founded the first legal distillery at the site. Archibald Campbell constructed another and the two combined to become Lagavulin. Lagavulin is originator of the famous blend, 'White Horse.'

Lagavulin has won four consecutive gold medals at the San Francisco World Spirits competition between 2005-2008, and it has a high quality reputation.

LAGAVULIN AND THE LAW

Records show illicit distillation in at least ten illegal distillers as far back as 1742. It was well into the 19th Century when arrangements to collect duty here fell into line with those applying elsewhere in Scotland. In the 19th century several legal battles took place between Lagavulin and neighbouring distillery, Laphraoig.

Lagavulin 16 Year Old

NOSE

Smoky, tannins, spicy, sherry and vanilla.

TASTE

Malty, sherry, sweet, peaty and oaky.

APPEARANCE

Old gold.

BELL'S

ENTERPRISING

In 1825 a small shop opened in Perth, Scotland. Among other things, it sold whisky. One enterprising salesman, Arthur Bell, quickly realised the potential of blended whisky. He travelled around Scotland and the Isles to find malt whiskies for his own blends, making it his aim to source well-aged spirit. Bell believed that a good blend of fine whiskies was better than a single malt. His sons joined him to form a family business.

It wasn't until 1904 that the name 'Arthur Bell and Sons' appeared on his first bottles of blended whisky. It is still made from 35 different whiskies, which are matured for between five and 12 years.

AFORE YE GO

In 1925 the company registered the motto, 'Afore ye go.' The slogan came about in the First World War, when cases of Bell's were sent to the docks for soldiers to enjoy, before going to war.

At the end of the American Prohibition, Bell's took on a further three distilleries, including Blair Athol, which had started life as a farm and is now the distillery's home. In 1978 Bell's became the official UK's number one whisky.

Bell's Original

NOSE

Cereal, honey, malty, barley and herbs.

TASTE

Barley, cereal, nut oils, woody and spicy.

APPEARANCE

Golden yellow.

BALVENIE

HISTORY

The Balvenie is a Scotch whisky produced in Dufftown, Scotland, just underneath the Glenfiddich Distillery. The Balvenie Distillery was built in 1892 by William Grant, who began to learn the art of distilling as a book-keeper at the Mortlach Distillery in 1866. Grant was born in Dufftown in 1839 in his father's house, and by the age of seven was sent out to herd cattle in order to augment the family income. Grant later bought a field close to the Balvenie Castle and building began in 1886. The first distillation process took place in May 1893.

UNIQUE FLAVOUR

Although The Balvenie shares its water supply with that of the Glenfiddich Distillery – the Robbie Dhu Springs – its flavour is remarkably different. It is one of the few Scotch distilleries to boast of its own traditional malting floor, and also grows its own crop and barley. The Balvenie DoubleWood 12 Year Old gains its distinctive flavour through its maturation in two different wooden casks. The Balvenie use different cask types and ages in order to develop unique flavours and new interpretations of the classic character.

Balvenie DoubleWood 12 Year Old

NOSE

A sweet fruitiness, with honey, vanilla and sherry.

TASTE

Nutty, with notes of cinnamon and sherry flavours, and a long, warm finish.

APPEARANCE

Amber.

JOHNNIE WALKER

SCOTLAND

ABOUT

FROM HUMBLE BEGINNINGS

Johnnie Walker started in Kilmarnock, Scotland.
John Walker (a fourteen year old) started to sell whisky
in his grocery store, a shop he had inherited on the death
of his father. The whisky grew in popularity and Walker's
family continued the business. In 1887 branches opened
in South Africa and the whisky has since become the most
widely distributed Scotch in the world, with the company
currently expanding into China. In 2011, the brand sold
over 1 million cases in the USA, Brazil and Thailand. It
sold more than 500,000 cases in Mexico and Australia.
In 1934 Johnnie Walker received its first Royal Warrant -
remaining suppliers to the royal household to this day.

BOTTLE ARTWORK

In 1903 cartoonist Tom Browne sketched the 'Striding
Man' on the back of a menu card. It became the official
artwork found on Johnnie Walker bottles, still used today.

CHURCHILLIAN CONNECTIONS

Winston Churchill created a painting called 'Bottlescape',
which still hangs at Chartwell, in honour of his favourite
drink – Johnnie Walker Black Label.

Johnnie Walker Black Label 12 Year Old

NOSE

Spices, treacle, peppery and citrus.

TASTE

Smoky, spicy, barley, cereal, toffee and herbs.

APPEARANCE

Deep gold.

FAMOUS GROUSE

SCOTLAND

ABOUT

HISTORY

Matthew Gloag was a grocer and wine merchant in Perth. When Queen Victoria visited Perth in 1842, Gloag was invited to supply the wines for the Royal Banquet. He also bought whiskies from Scottish distilleries. Eighteen years later, his son took over the company and began producing blended whiskies. In 1896, William's nephew, Matthew, who was named after his grandfather, took over the company. It was Matthew who created The Grouse blend in the same year. It became so popular, it was renamed 'The Famous Grouse.' Matthew's daughter, Phillippa, designed the first Grouse label. The company remained in family ownership until 1970.

By 1980 The Famous Grouse had become the highest selling whisky in Scotland. It now sells over two million cases globally and in 1984 was awarded the Royal Warrant.

BLENDED QUALITY

Single malt whiskies used in The Famous Grouse include Highland Park and The Macallan. The blend is matured in oak casks for up to six months. The Famous Grouse's symbol is the red grouse, Scotland's national game bird.

Famous Grouse
Blended Scotch Whisky

NOSE

Barley, toffee, light and floral.

TASTE

Spices, barley, caramel and lightly smoky.

APPEARANCE

Golden, bright.

GRANT'S

SCOTLAND

ABOUT

HISTORY

Grant's is a blended Scottish whisky. In 1886
William Grant started work as a book-keeper in
a whisky distillery. Three years later the largest
Scottish whisky blender at the time, called
Pattison's, went bust. William Grant spotted an
opportunity. He stepped in and decided to launch
his own blended whisky.

One of Grant's son-in-laws, Charles Gordon,
became the company's first salesman. He took
Grant's blended whisky to Australia and the Far
East in 1909. The company remains family-run and
Grant's is the oldest family-owned blended whisky
on the market. It sells in 180 countries world-wide.

TRIANGULAR BOTTLES

In 1957 Grant's was sold in an unusual triangular
bottle. The company wanted a design that would
showcase the quality and colour of the whisky, as
well as being able to be stacked and shipped easily.

Grant's Blended Scotch Whisky The Family Reserve

NOSE

Clean, sweet, some fruitiness and malt.

TASTE

Vanilla, sweets and malty sharpness.

APPEARANCE

Golden.

47

Although Scotland is famed for its vast production of whisky, Bushmills Distillery in Ireland claims to be the oldest whisky distillery in the world. Ireland struggled with whisky production for decades due to tax, abstinence and war, but has since become one of the most famous whisky-producing countries in the world.

ORIGINS OF IRISH WHISKY

IN THE BEGINNING

It is widely accepted that Celtic Christian monks, who encountered the principals of distillation in Moorish Spain, put this new-found technique of alcohol distillation to use in Ireland. Distillation was applied in countries using the local produce – for example, barley. Until 1600, Ireland was ruled by Irish chieftains, who operated until Celtic law systems. The English tried to introduce licensing and tax systems, but were unsuccessful, as their control only really reached to Dublin, so distilling remained independent of English legislation.

At the time, distilling was a cottage industry with hundreds of home-based distilleries throughout the country. Distilling whisky was part of everyday country life, like butter-making or meat curing. This changed in 1601 with the ill-fated Spanish invasion at the Battle of Kinsale (Co. Cork), the subsequent Flight of the Earls and the collapse of the old Gaelic order. The English conquest of Ireland now meant an English tax system could be introduced, whereby distillers needed a license to operate. By 1608 the first distillery licence was granted to Charles Waterhouse in Munster.

IRISH WHISKY GOES GLOBAL

Just ten years later, Richard Boyle, the first Earl of Cork and a personal friend of Sir Walter Raleigh, noted in his diary for 20th March, 1617 a gift of whisky, which would accompany Raleigh to America.

The reputation of Irish liquor grew. In 1682, Peter the Great of Russia declared - "of all wines, the Irish wine is best".

The imposition of English malt taxes throughout the 18th century caused Irish distillers to look for ways to avoid paying tax – one inventive solution was to create Pot Still Irish whisky. The Irish distillers found that adding 'green' barley also gave a surprisingly good taste.

INVENTION, CREATION AND CONTROVERSY

By the late 1700s, the Industrial Revolution had arrived in the main cities of Ireland and the Irish whisky distilling industry embraced all of the advantages which it presented. Many of the large Irish whisky houses grew in this time, including Jameson's. By 1835, the number of distilleries in Ireland had grown to 93 and the largest pot-still in the world was in operation at Midleton Distillery, Cork.

In 1830, the former Inspector General of Excise in Ireland, Aeneas Coffey, filed a patent for a new invention for what was to revolutionise the distilling industry worldwide. Coffey invented a new continuous distillation process which would be more efficient and quicker. However, these new 'patent' or 'coffey' stills were shunned by the Irish distillers who didn't like the spirit it produced. Finding no buyers for his invention in Ireland, Coffey moved to Scotland where he was welcomed by a growing whisky industry. Coffey's invention particularly suited new, blended whisky styles.

ABSTINENCE

Irish whisky was further hit by a new trend in the 1830s – abstinence. As poverty gripped the country, many drowned their sorrows in drink. A capuchin friar from County Cork, Father Theobald Matthew, started his 'total abstinence' campaign as a result. In just five years over five million of a population of eight million Irish citizens had taken "the pledge". That same year, 20 distilleries closed.

Next was the Great Famine in 1847. Following a series of failed potato crops, over one million Irish citizens died and another million emigrated to America.

ARGUMENTS OVER DEFINITIONS

In the 1850s tax laws were changed so that tax would be paid on shipment rather than on production of whisky spirit. This meant that whisky could be purchased and put in 'bond' with no up-front taxation charges. This gave a commercial advantage to Scottish distilleries. Entrepreneurs in other fields were able to bring their business acumen to whisky, often producing blended whiskies in high volume and with cheaper price tags. The Irish war on other forms of whisky production continued with the publication of a book 'The Truth About Whisky'. In the book four leading pot still distillers sought to discredit other forms of whisky production, arguing that anything other than pot still production wasn't rightfully whisky.

Globally Irish pot still whisky continued to do well. An unfortunate insect plague devastated French cognac-producing vineyards (Cognac being a main competitor for whisky), which had a positive impact on Irish whisky production. Big Irish Distilleries such as Jameson and Powers employed hundreds of workers and had on-site cooperages, stables, blacksmiths and carpenters for the whole production process. At this time, they introduced the alternative spelling for Irish whisky – with an extra 'e'.

The argument with Scottish production methods continued. Scotland's largest distillery in the 1900s, DCL, set up its own Irish distillery in Dublin. To settle the argument once and for all, the 'Royal Commission on Whisky and other Potable Spirits' was set up. It took a year and a half to declare that whisk(e)y from patent stills was still whisky. The Irish had lost their argument. The Scottish Coffey-stills producing whisky flooded the market and whisky prices collapsed. Added to this, Ireland found itself in the grip of recession and the beginning of World War 1. 1916 brought the turbulent Easter Rising and by 1917 all barley production in Ireland had been diverted to the war effort.

By 1920 the Irish were losing ground to Scottish whisky even in America, traditionally a stronghold of Irish whisky and Prohibition virtually cut off all export of Irish whisky.

WAR AT HOME

Troubles at home didn't help. The Irish War of Independence in 1921 and the Irish Civil War from 1922-23 both had negative impacts on Irish whisky production, whilst Scottish distilleries, at peace, were able to forge ahead with production and building their brands overseas. By the time Prohibition ended in 1933, the Irish whisky industry was in no position to take advantage of the new demand. And in 1932, to make matters even worse, a tussle with its largest trading partner, Great Britain, resulted in Ireland being shut out of 25% of world markets, with any remaining export options difficult to access. By 1948 there were a mere three distillers in the Republic of Ireland and three in Northern Ireland. Just five years later, only five survived – Jameson, Powers and Cork Distilleries Company (CDC) in the ROI and Bushmills and Coleraine in Northern Ireland.

TURNING THE CORNER

Fortunes for Irish whisky began to change when Jameson and CDC merged in 1966 to form Irish Distillers Ltd.

Irish whisky production finally embraced new whisky production technology, with Irish Distillers Ltd opening a new state-of-the-art distillery in Cork in 1975. It remains one of the most advanced distilleries in the world. This has led to a revival of interest in Irish whisky, particularly pot-still whiskies and this is an area of whisky that looks likely to grow once again.

BUSHMILLS

HISTORY

Bushmills Distillery is on the north coast of County Antrim, Northern Ireland. Bushmills claims to be the oldest whisky distillery in the world. As far back as 1276, it is recorded that Sir Robert Savage of Ards fortified his troops before battle with a 'mighty drop of aqua vitae', which was then the popular name for whisky.

Bushmills Distillery was founded in 1608, when King James 1 granted Sir Thomas Phillips, landowner and Governor of country Antrim, a license to distil. Bushmills Old Distillery Company was established in 1784 by Hugh Anderson and the Pot Still became its trademark. Despite the introduction of a new malt tax in 1850, which caused some distillers to change their recipes, Bushmills didn't. In 1885, a disastrous fire destroyed Bushmills distillery, but a mere four years later it won a Gold Medal at the Paris 1889 Expo.

Bushmills 10 Year Old

NOSE

Banana, green apples, vanilla and a touch of caramel.

TASTE

Fruity, chocolate, peas, apples, vanilla and fudge.

APPEARANCE

Golden Amber.

GREENORE

ABOUT

HISTORY

The Port of Greenore is located a few miles from Cooley Distillery in County Louth, Ireland. The grain used to make this whisky was shipped into Greenore Port – hence the name. The distillery itself was converted in 1987 from an older potato alcohol plant by John Teeling. In 2011, US drinks company Beam Inc bought Cooley for around €70 million.

Greenore is made from maize, corn and is made in a single distillery – which is why it's called a single grain whisky. Greenore Single Grain is aged for a minimum of eight years in casks that once held bourbon. The bourbon casks give the whisky rich oaky and sweet flavours. Unlike other Irish whiskies, which are usually distilled three times, Cooley's products are distilled twice (it's thought that the third distillation can remove some of the flavours).

AWARDS

Greenore has won best in class three years running (from 2008-2010) at the International Wine and Spirits Competition. Fans of the whisky describe its taste as having honey or toffee tones. Cooley has won over 300 medals since opening.

Greenore 8 Year Old

NOSE

Crisp, honey, spicy, sweet and with cereals.

TASTE

Dry, soft, honey, toffee, spicy with a hint of vanilla.

APPEARANCE

Pale yellow.

JAMESON

HISTORY

John Jameson was born in October 1740. His family's motto was 'sine metu' (without fear), which was awarded to them for their bravery in fighting pirates on the high seas in the 1500s. Thirty years later this motto inspired Jameson to move to Dublin to start a whisky distillery. Jameson was convinced that quality ingredients would make his whisky successful – so he personally chose the barley and casks, insisting that his whisky was distilled three times, not twice like Scottish whisky.

Jameson was also an ethical employer – workers at the distillery enjoyed the best wages and working conditions in the city. He also believed in sharing his time and profits with them. The Jameson label features two barrel-men balancing the label, in tribute to the hard workers at the Jameson Distillery.

FAMILY & FRIENDS

By 1810 John Jameson's son, John II, had expanded the distillery. Now it was the second largest in Ireland. Eventually it became one of the most well-known whiskies in the world, known under the name 'John Jameson and Sons Whisky.' The original John Jameson died aged 83.

Jameson Irish Whiskey

NOSE

Madeira, grass, marmalade, fudge in a smooth sweetness.

TASTE

Fruity, fresh, vanilla and creamy.

APPEARANCE

Light honey and pale gold.

ABOUT

HISTORY

In 1757 Matthias Manus founded the Kilbeggan Distillery on the banks of the River Brosna. Kilbeggan comes from the Gaelic for 'church of Becan' and is situated in Moycashel, County Westmeath, Ireland. In 1794 the Codd family made a stake in the distillery. They wanted to expand it and increase its capacity. The distillery grew thanks to a new branch of the Grand Canal, which was extended into Kilbeggan and which made transportation relatively easy. Just four families in total have operated the Kilbeggan distillery since its beginnings in the 1800s – they are the McManus family, the Codd family, the Locke family and the Teeling family.

Kilbeggan

NOSE

Nutty, oily, barley, cereal and a hint of peat.

TASTE

Honey and malty with a touch of oak.

APPEARANCE

Rich gold.

MIDLETON

IRELAND

ABOUT

HISTORY

Midleton is a premium blended Irish whisky. It's produced by Irish Distillers Group in Midleton, a town in East Cork, Ireland, the same distillery that produces Jameson whisky – although it's now owned by Pernod-Ricard. Irish Distillers was formed in 1966, when a merger took place between Irish whisky distillers John Power & Son, John Jameson & Son and the Cork Distillery Company. In July 1975 production ended at the Old Midleton Distillery and began again in the morning at the new Midleton complex. The old site has since opened as a visitor centre.

The Midleton factory has a production capacity of 19 million litres per year and is the biggest in Ireland.

SHOWCASING BLENDS

Midleton Very Rare whisky was launched in 1984 to celebrate the whiskies produced at Midleton. A new vintage is released very year. Every bottle is individually numbered and is also signed by the master distiller. Only 50 casks are released every year which makes it a premium-priced, collectors' whisky.

Midleton Barry Crockett Legacy

NOSE

Barley, floral, honey, rosemary, hay, citrus, toffee and apples.

TASTE

Toffee, honey, vanilla, sweet candied peel, with a touch of cinnamon.

APPEARANCE

Pale gold.

ABOUT

HISTORY

Redbreast is a type of single pot still Irish whisky. It is produced at the New Midleton Distillery by Irish Distillers, a subsidiary of Pernod-Ricard. Redbreast is one of very few single pot still whiskies produced today.

In 1857 a company called W & A Gilbey founded and began to trade out of a basement in cellars on the corner of Oxford Street in London. Successful from the start, Gilbey's soon had branches in Dublin, Belfast and Edinburgh. In 1866 the company moved to new stores in Dublin, which contained their own vaults, tasting room and a small still. By 1874 Gilbey's held in bond of over 300,000 gallons of whisky from 'the most celebrated Dublin Distilleries.' In 1875 they sold 83,000 casks of Irish whisky. By the mid-1960s, Redbreast was being bottled in batches of 18,000 litres a year. 1985 was the last year Redbreast was bottled under Gilbey's. In 1991 it was re-introduced by Irish Distillers after a ten-year absence.

Redbreast 12 Year Old

NOSE

Nutty, fruity, oily with dried peels.

TASTE

Marzipan, peels, sherry, nuts, citrus, custard and spices.

APPEARANCE

Medium amber.

ABOUT

HISTORY

In 1829 the Tullamore Distillery was founded in Tullamore, County Offaly by Michael Molloy – an area rich in grain growing. Following the death of Molloy in 1887, the distillery was taken over by Captain Bernard Daly. He left the day-to-day running of the distillery to his colleague, Daniel E Williams. Williams was a man who had a major influence on the development of the distillery and his initials – D.E.W. – form the Dew part of Tullamore-Dew. The original slogan – 'give every man his Dew' – is still used today.

Williams brought electricity to Tullamore in 1893 and also installed the town's first telephones, as well as encouraging motorised transport. Entrepreneurial by nature, he ran a drinks business, imported tea, sold seed and grain and had a network of 26 general stores.

IRISH WOLFHOUNDS

Desmond Williams, grandson of Daniel Williams, felt that the Irish wolfhound was a good symbol for his whisky and reflected the character of the Irish people, with associations of loyalty, heritage, strength and friendship. Williams was himself a breeder of Irish wolfhounds. In the 1950s he included two wolfhounds and a harp to the label of Tullamore Dew. They remain on the label today.

Tullamore-Dew

NOSE

Caramel, toffee, sweet, fruity, biscuity and peels.

TASTE

Butter, honey, vanilla cream, grains, sherried peels, spices and a hint of caramel sweetness.

APPEARANCE

Light gold.

ABOUT

HISTORY

Connemara comes from the wild region of Connemara in Ireland. It's situated on Ireland's Atlantic Coast in county Galway. Famous for its natural beauty, Connemara has the Twelve Ben mountain range, along with peat boglands and scenic lakes. The pure water and peated boglands of Connemara helped to give the whisky from this region its distinctive taste. Connemara is made in the Cooley distillery in county Cork, using pure spring water from the Cooley Mountains and peated, malted barley.

MORE'S THE PEATY

Connemara is unusual for Irish whiskies in that it has a peaty taste, more often associated with Scottish whisky. Unlike most other Irish whiskies, Connemara is double distilled in two small pot stills and then left to mature in oak casks. Its distinctive taste comes from drying malting barley over peat fires. The smoke that rises through the malted barley during this drying process lends a smoky flavour and aroma to the final spirit.

Connemara Peated

NOSE

Smoky, peaty, heather, fresh, floral, honey and woody.

TASTE

Malt, peat, honey, smoke and barley.

APPEARANCE

Light gold.

TYRCONNELL

ABOUT

HISTORY

The Tyrconnell is a brand of Irish whisky that was previously owned by the Watt Distillery and dates back to 1762. The Watt family had a tradition of producing good whisky, as well as a reputation for horse racing. The Tyrconnell was their main product and is, in fact, named after a successful race-horse that the family owned.

The Tyrconnell was revived by the Cooley Distillery. It's made from 100% malted barley in traditional copper pot stills.

TYRCONNELL AND A HORSE

In 1876 the Watt family entered a chestnut colt, named 'The Tyrconnell' into the Irish classic horse race called 'The National Produce Stakes.' Against odds of 100 to 1, the horse won a spectacular victory. This win inspired the Watt Distillery to celebrate the occasion by creating a special commemorative Tyrconnell label – this remains in use to this day.

Tyrconnell Irish Whiskey

Fruity sweet, malty, crisp, oaky and oily.

Barley, malt, buttery, grains, honey and a little spice.

APPEARANCE

Golden yellow.

ABOUT

HISTORY

The Powers Distillery was founded in 1791 by James Power in the John's Lane area of Dublin, near the Western Gate of Dublin City. At the turn of the 19th Century in 1809, James Power's son, John, joined the company and led it to great success under the name John Power & Sons, a limited company. As the distillery's popularity grew, so did the stature of the Power family. John Power was knighted, and later made the High Sheriff of Dublin, in recognition of his hard work and success.

In 1871 the distillery was rebuilt in Victorian Style, occupying 7 acres (28,000 m2) of land and employing around 300 people. It became one of the most impressive sights in Dublin.

BOTTLING THE GOLD LABEL

Powers Distillery was the first in Ireland – and one of the first in the world - to start bottling whisky, rather than selling it in the cask. It was adorned with a gold label, earning the whisky the famous 'Gold Label' name. The label promised a higher quality whisky, and distinguished it from other, white-labelled bottles. Powers was also the first distillery in the world to produce miniature bottles, known as 'Baby Powers', in 1920. An act of parliament was required in order for Powers to launch its 71ml bottles.

Powers is now one of the best-selling whiskys in Ireland, although it hasn't earned as much popularity in the rest of the world. The company remained under family ownership until 1966, when Powers joined with the Cork Distillers Company and John Jameson & Sons to form the Irish Distillers Group. Now, international company Pernod-Ricard owns the Irish Distillers.

Powers 12 Year Old

NOSE

Full-bodied and flavoursome, honey, spices with a hint of perfumed oils.

TASTE

Smooth and spicy, with hints of wood.

APPEARANCE

Golden amber.

THE USA

American whisky is whisky that is produced in the
United States from a fermented mash of cereal grain.

USA

TYPES OF WHISKY

Rye whisky is a type of whisky, which is made from mash that consists of at least 51% rye. Rye malt whisky is made from a mash that contains at least 51% malted rye. Malt whisky is made from a mash that contains at least 51% malted barley and wheat whisky is made from a mash that consists of at least 51% wheat. Bourbon whisky, on the other hand, comes from mash that consists of at least 51% corn maize and corn whisky has an even higher percentage of maize mash origins at least 80%.

US whisky rules stipulate that, unless a whisky is blended, it must not be more than 80% alcohol by volume to maintain the flavour of the original mash. Adding colouring, caramel or other flavourings is also not allowed. All types of American whisky, except for corn whisky, must be aged and they must be aged in new, charred oak containers. American corn whisky does not have to be aged, but if it is aged, it must be done in used or uncharred oak barrels – often it's done in used bourbon barrels (which are also used by other distilleries in the world).

Straight whisky is whisky that's not more than 80% alcohol by volume and has been aged for at least two years, but has no other added colourings or flavourings. 'Straight' can be added to the definition of the whisky – as in 'straight rye whisky'. Blended whisky is a mixture that contains straight whisky or a blend of straight whiskys, as well as other permissible ingredients.

A specific class of American whisky is Tennessee whisky. Types of Tennessee whisky include Jack Daniel's, George Dickel and Jailers. These brands often use a filtering stage, which is called the 'Lincoln Count Process.' In this process, whisky is filtered through a thick layer of maple charcoal, before being put into casks for ageing.

HISTORY

One of the key moments in the history of American whisky production was the 'Whisky Rebellion' (or whisky insurrection), which began in 1791. This was a protest against the introduction of new taxes and began under the presidency of George Washington.

Until the tax, farmers had used their leftover grain and corn to make whisky, which they used as a form of exchange. Under the new – and unpopular legislation – such exchanges were now to be taxed. The tax was part of treasury secretary, Alexander Hamilton's, program to increase government power and centralise control. Bitter debates between farmers and politicians ensued. The farmers argued that they were fighting for the principles of the American Revolution, which would have been against taxation without local representation. Whilst the central Government argued that the taxes were a legitimate expression of the powers of Congress.

The debate became so bitter, that there were violent clashes between protestors and federal officials, who came to try to collect the tax. Things came to a climax in July 1794, when a state marshal came to Pennsylvania to service writs against distillers who had not paid the duty. As a result, more than 500 men attacked the home of tax inspector General John Neville. Washington then sent in peace commissioners to negotiate with the protestors, as well as 13,000 men who had been provided by the governors of Virginia, Maryland, New Jersey and Pennsylvania to quash the rebellion.

The whisky tax was finally repealed in 1800, when Thomas Jefferson's Republican Party successfully came into power.

PROHIBITION

One period of American history had a huge impact on whisky production, not just on home soil, but worldwide, too. That was Prohibition. During Prohibition, the manufacture and sale of alcohol was made illegal. Drinking itself was not illegal and there were exceptions for medicinal and religious use. Prohibition in America was part of the reform movement from 1840s to the 1920s and was sponsored by evangelical Protestant churches, especially Methodists, Baptists, Presbyterians, Disciples and Congregationalists. The Women's Christian Temperance Movement was founded in 1874. There was nationwide prohibition during World War I. As well as a ban on making alcohol, there was a ban on imports and exports. Nationwide prohibition was finally repealed at the end of 1933 and states were then free to set their own laws to control alcohol.

REGIONS OF WHISKY PRODUCTION

Whisky has played an important role in the economy and culture of the American colonies and the early United States. As early as 1657, Boston had a rum distillery. Whisky production was the preferred way to convert surplus grain into a saleable product. It was brought to America by European farmers who emigrated and who made whisky from whatever local grains were available. Corn was particularly popular, since it was in ready supply. In fact, there was such a glut of it in the Corn Belt in Kentucky and Ohio, that it was more economical to convert it into a liquid asset.

States such as Pennsylvania, Maryland and Virginia have a whisky-making heritage, especially Kentucky for Bourbon and Tennessee whisky.

BOURBON

WHAT IS IT?

Bourbon whisky is a type of American whisky made from corn. It's aged in barrels. Its name comes from its association with an area known as 'Old Bourbon', which is now Bourbon County in Kentucky. Originally the name 'bourbon' came from the royal French House of Bourbon.

HISTORY

Bourbon has been produced since the 1700s and is strongly associated with the American South, in particular Kentucky. By 1964 US Congress recognised bourbon whisky as a 'distinctive product of the United Sates.' It's possible to make it anywhere in the US, but most brands are produced in Kentucky. In fact, 97% of all bourbon is distilled and aged somewhere near Bardstown, Kentucky, affectionately known as the 'bourbon capital of the world.' Bardstown is also home to an annual Bourbon Festival, which is held each September. The Kentucky Distillers' Association estimates that there are almost five million barrels of bourbon aging in Kentucky at any one time. That means more bottles of bourbon than there are people in the state of Kentucky!

WHERE DID IT COME FROM?

The invention of bourbon is often given to Elijah Craig, a Baptists minister. It's Craig who is credited with aging the distillation in charred oak casks, which is said to give bourbon its unique colour and taste. This may however only be a legend, as the true roots of bourbon creation are not clear. Distilling probably arrived in Kentucky with Scottish and other settlers, who would have brought the skills of whisky making with them from their home countries and applied the techniques to common materials to hand in their new land.

BOURBON TRAIL

The Kentucky Bourbon Trail takes in seven distilleries in the state: Four Roses, Heaven Hill, Jim Beam, Maker's Mark, Town Branch, Wild Turkey and Woodford Reserve.

RYE WHISKY

WHAT IS IT?

Rye whisky must be made from a mash of at least 51% rye. The other ingredients of rye mash are usually corn and malted barley, but could be wheat or malted rye, too. Other experimental ingredients include rice, oats and other grains. It is aged in new, charred oak barrels. The newness of the barrels also lends distinctive flavour to the spirit. So-called 'straight rye' must meet the legal requirements of normal rye, but it must also be aged at least two years and may contain no added flavouring, colourings or additional spirits. If a distillery blends several barrels of rye to make a batch for bottling, it will include the age of the youngest barrel on the bottle.

Rye gives a spicy or fruity flavour to traditional whisky flavours. This comes from the use of virgin oak in the production process. Rye whisky can be compared to a Scottish Islay whisky.

WHERE DOES IT COME FROM?

Rye whisky was the main whisky of the north-eastern states, especially Pennsylvania and Maryland. Prohibition in the late 1800s and early 1900s all but wiped out rye whisky, although a few brands, such as Old Overholt, survived. Today Heaven Hill, Four Roses, Jim Beam, Bulleit, Knob Creek and Catoctin are some current producers of rye whisky.

WHAT'S THE DIFFERENCE BETWEEN RYE AND BOURBON?

Rye gives a spicy or fruity flavour to traditional whisky flavours. This comes from the use of virgin oak in the production process. Rye whisky can be compared to a Scottish Islay whisky. Bourbon tends to be sweeter and more full-bodied than rye whisky. Originally cocktails such as Whisky Sours, Manhattans and Old Fashioneds were made with rye, which relied on the rustic spirit, although these cocktails are now also made with bourbon.

CORN WHISKY

WHAT IS IT?

Corn whisky is sometimes known as 'corn liquor', 'white dog' or 'white lightning.' It does not have the amber colours of traditional whiskies. It's made from a mash of at least 80% corn. It is based on typical American moonshine, which was a type of whisky made illegally with corn (and often some sugar). Nowadays commercial operators, such as Heaven Hill and Buffalo Trace, produce corn whiskys for sale. High proof whisky is diluted with water to reach a lower alcohol per volume percentage – often around 40-60%.

Corn whisky may be aged in uncharred oak barrels, but the process is usually quick – around six months or less. During this time, the corn whisky absorbs colour and flavour from the barrels.

Straight corn whisky is aged for longer – typically in used or uncharred new oak barrels for two years or more.

WHERE IS IT MADE?

Corn whisky has its roots firmly in home-made territory and is most often associated with independent makers. For example, Thirteenth Century is a small distillery in Americus, Georgia. It produces small batches of corn whisky. Its Southern Corn Whisky has been awarded Gold Medal at the 2011 World Spirits Competition and San Francisco Spirits Competition.

However, in 2012 big whisky producer Jack Daniel's produced its first 'white dog' unaged rye whisky, made since the prohibition era. It is made with a combination of 70% rye, 18% corn and 12% malted barley. It still goes through the Jack Daniels' charcoal mellowing process, like other bourbons produced by the distiller. There are rumours that Jack Daniels' is experimenting with other corn whiskies, too.

OLD THOMPSON

USA

ABOUT

HISTORY

Old Thompson is an American blended whisky. It is produced by Barton Brands, now owned by multinational Sazerac company. It is well-known for its low price. Old Thompson dates back to 1904, when it was introduced by the Glenmore Distillery Company, which was then owned by two brothers, James and Francis P. Thompson.

LOW COST, MINIMUM REQUIREMENTS

Old Thompson is made from neutral grain spirits and straight whiskies with the minimum percentage of straight whiskies required by American law (20%). It also has the minimum alcohol content (40%). The age statement on bottles of Old Thompson refers to the age of the straight whiskies it contains. In the case of Old Thompson that's four years – which means it has 20% straight whiskies that are four years old. There's no requirement to list the age of neutral grain spirits, which therefore may not have been aged. Some of the straight whisky used in Old Thompsons is bourbon.

Old Thompson American Whiskey

NOSE

Citrus, herbs and minerals.

TASTE

Tangy fruit with spices.

APPEARANCE

Dark, golden amber.

ELIJAH CRAIG

ABOUT

HISTORY

Elijah Craig is a bourbon whisky produced by the Heaven Hill Distillery Company. The headquarters for the company is in Bardstown, Kentucky, but the distillery itself is situated in Louisville, Kentucky, under the name Heaven Hill Bernheim Distillery. Elijah Craig is named so in honour of Reverend Elijah Craig, who was born in Virginia in the 18th century. Craig was a Baptist preacher and eventually educator and entrepreneur in the area of Virginia that later became Kentucky. Craig is credited with improving the locally-made liquor into something like the bourbon you taste today, by discovering the benefits of using fire-charred barrels during the ageing process, and is most widely known in association with this particular brand of bourbon.

HAND-PICKED

Elijah Craig is aged to a 12 year old expression, or a 20 year old. Elijah Craig 20 year old is in fact the oldest single barrel bourbon in the world that has been allowed to mature for this long. The 12 year old is a premium bourbon, and even gained this reputation before the term even existed. Elijah Craig is a critically acclaimed bourbon, having been award a double gold medal at the San Francisco World Spirits Competitions, and twice awarded 'Best of the Best' from Whisky Magazine.

Elijah Craig 12 Year Old

NOSE

Sweetness with notes of oak, toffee, spicy stewed fruits, and a creme anglaise character.

TASTE

Stewed Bramley apples, aniseed and a hint of spice. With a sweet, oak finish.

APPEARANCE

Golden caramel.

JACK DANIEL'S

HISTORY

Jack Daniel's is a brand of sour mash Tennessee whisky. It's the most popular American whisky in the world, with a distinctive square bottle and black label. It is produced in Lynchburg, Tennessee by the Jack Daniel Distillery.

Jasper 'jack' Daniel was born in 1846 and became a licensed distiller around the age of twenty years old. Jack had eleven siblings. His grandfather had emigrated from Wales to the United States with his Scottish grandmother. The family business continued with Jack's nephew, Lem Motlow, who subsequently gave it to his own children.

MAPLE FILTERING AND AGEING

Jack Daniel's is filtered through sugar maple charcoal in large vats before being aged. This is an extra step that is not used in making most bourbon whisky. Barrels that have been used for Jack Daniel's have been used by other companies to make Tabasco sauce and rum.

DRY COUNTY

The distillery itself is located in Moore County, which is a dry county that does not allow the purchase of alcohol. However it is legal to produce it within the county. In addition, a distillery may sell one commemorative product – Jack Daniels', now sells two blends in its shop.

Jack Daniel's Tennessee Whiskey

NOSE

Dry spices, oils, nuts, touch of smoke and light and smooth.

TASTE

Banana, milk, nuts, caramel, crème anglaise and a touch of oakiness.

APPEARANCE

Light gold.

ABOUT

HISTORY

Jim Beam is a type of American bourbon whisky. It is one of the best-selling brands of bourbon in the world. Since 1795 seven generations of the Beam family have been involved in the whisky production. It was given the name 'Jim Beam' in 1933 in honour of James Beam, who rebuilt the business after Prohibition.

The Beams were originally the 'Boehms', who emigrated from Germany and changed their name. Johannes Beam, a farmer, began producing bourbon in the 1790s at a distillery called 'Old Tub.' David Beam took over his father's responsibilities in 1820, aged 18 and grew the distribution.

The Jim Beam bourbon brand is now owned and produced by Beam Inc, a company formed in 2011. Beam has its headquarters in Chicago.

POST- PROHIBITION YEAST

Jim Beam is made with water filtered through the limestone rocks in central Kentucky. A strain of yeast used since the end of Prohibition is added and the mash is gradually created. Old mash is also used in the traditional 'sour mash' process.

Jim Beam White Label

NOSE

Cereal, vanilla, hay, corn and a touch of sweetness.

TASTE

Oaky, vanilla, crème anglaise, spicy and peppery.

APPEARANCE

Pale straw.

FOUR ROSES

HISTORY

Four Roses is a Kentucky straight bourbon whisky. It was established in 1888, when Paul Jones Junior moved his business to Louisville, Kentucky and opened an office in a section of the historic Main Street, which was known as 'whisky row'. Four years later he trademarked the name 'Four Roses' and in 1922 the Paul Jones Company bought the Frankfort Distilling Company. It was the top selling bourbon in the United States in the 1930s, 1940s and 1950s and was owned by Seagram from 1943. Despite its popularity, Seagram decided to stop selling Four Roses in America, as they wanted to concentrate on blended whisky. Four Roses marketing focused more on Europe and Asia, which were growing markets at the time.

At the same time, however, the Four Roses name was used in the States for blended whisky, although not as a straight bourbon. It took 40 years to reappear on American shelves as a straight bourbon, when the business had changed hands and the brand was bought by Vivendi, who subsequently sold to Diageo and then to the Kirin Brewery Company of Japan. Things came full circle again when Kirin discontinued sales of blended whisky and concentrated instead on Four Roses as a straight bourbon whisky.

Four Roses Bourbon

Sweet, crisp, marmalade, citrus, sweet, toffee and a touch of caramel.

Citrus, honey, cereal, spicy, lemonade with oaky hints.

Bright amber.

ABOUT

HISTORY

Wild Turkey is a type of Kentucky straight bourbon whisky. Its distillery is near Lawrenceburg, Kentucky. In 1855 Austin Nichols started to sell wine and spirits as a wholesale grocer. The business he owned would later own Wild Turkey bourbon. The Ripy brothers built a distillery in Tyrone, Kentucky, near to Lawrenceburg in 1869 on Wild Turkey Hill. They consolidated it in the early 1900s and resumed distilling after the end of Prohibition. Distillery executive, Thomas McCarthy, took some warehouse samples on a wild turkey hunting trip with some friends in 1940. The next year, his friends asked for 'some of that wild turkey whisky' – and so Wild Turkey bourbon was born.

WILD REPUTATION

Wild Turkey has something of a reputation in some quarters and one of the company's advertising campaigns has controversially included the slogan 'give 'em the bird', referring to a rude gesture. In 2012, master distiller of Wild Turkey, Jimmy Russell, called for US President Barack Obama to 'give us the bird.' Russell was referring to the fate of the traditional Thanksgiving Day turkey at the White House. Russell has been master distiller for over 50 years.

Wild Turkey 101

NOSE

Toffee, sweetness, oak, vanilla, creamy, zesty citrus and butterscotch.

TASTE

Pepper, caramel, grains, buttery, honey and sweet spiciness.

APPEARANCE

Pale gold.

MAKER'S MARK

HISTORY

Maker's Mark is a small batch bourbon whisky which is distilled in Loretto, Kentucky. It's sold in distinctive bottles which are sealed with red wax. Maker's Mark began production in 1954, after William 'Bill' Samuels Senior bought the distillery, known as 'Burks' Distillery' in Loretto for $35,000. 'Maker's Mark' has changed business hands many times –from Hiram Walker and Sons and Allied Domecq in the 1980s to Fortune Brands and Beam Inc more recently.

The first bottle of Maker's Mark was available in 1958. In the 1960s and 1970s Maker's Mark was marketed under the slogan, 'It tastes expensive… and it is.' After Bill Samuels Senior oversaw creation of the brand in the 1950s, its production was overseen by Bill Samuels Junior, his son, until 2011, when Samuels Jnr announced his retirement aged 70. However his son, Rob Samuels, succeeded him in 2011 to carry on the family interest.

BARREL ROTATION

Marker's Mark is aged for between five and seven years, and then bottled when company tasters agree that it is ready. The distillery is one of few that rotate their barrels from upper to lower levels during the ageing process. This is thought to even the temperature variations that occur between the upper floors and lower floors and ensures consistent quality and taste.

Maker's Mark

NOSE

Fruity, honey, spices, mixed peels, fruit and a touch of oak.

TASTE

Rye, spices, barley, malty, nutty, oily and hints of butterscotch and vanilla.

APPEARANCE

Amber-orange.

KENTUCKY GENTLEMAN

USA

ABOUT

HISTORY

Kentucky Gentleman is a bourbon whisky produced in Bardstown, Kentucky. The Sazerac Company owns it. The Sazerac Company is the largest distilling company in the United States. Its distilleries include Barton Distillery (in Bardstown, Kentucky), the Buffalo Trace Distillery (in Frankfort, Kentucky) and the A. Smith Bowman Distillery (in Fredericksburg, Virginia).

Kentucky Gentleman is sold both as a blend and as a straight bourbon. Its combination of bourbon and grain alcohol means it can be sold relatively cheap. Barton Brands of Kentucky currently produce the drink. The distillery was originally built in 1792 and now has a capacity for 20,000 barrels.

REPUTATION

Kentucky Gentleman has in some quarters a reputation for 'roughness', being seen as a drink for students or people who have fallen on hard times. Technically, because of its 51% content, it is a bourbon whisky, but experts occasionally dispute it as a drink of high quality. The company encourages visitors to its distillery, promising them that as they enter the ageing barrels warehouse, they will be greeted by a special, heady scent, which insiders call 'the angel's share'.

Kentucky Gentleman

NOSE

Fruity, roasted nuts, caramel.

TASTE

Cherry and oaky.

APPEARANCE

Medium amber.

BUFFALO TRACE

HISTORY

Buffalo Trace Distillery is the oldest distillery in the United States, located on what was once an ancient buffalo crossing on the banks of the Kentucky River in Franklin County. The distillery is named after the American bison that roamed the plains nearby. In 1792 Richard Taylor built 'Riverside' – a house that is on the distillery site today. In 1811 a three-story stone warehouse was constructed, to store goods for shipment, including whiske. Harrison Blanton constructed the first distillery on the site in 1812. In 1858 Daniel Swigert developed the site further and in 1870 Colonel Edmund Hayes Taylor Junior bought the distiller, calling it 'O.F.C' in reference to 'Old Fire Copper' and his belief that the best whisky was made in old-fashioned, wood-fired, copper stills. More investment from different owners continued.

EXPERT REVIEWS

Buffalo Trace is made from corn, rye and barley malt. It's aged in charred oak barrels. Around 30 barrels are selected and mixed before bottling. Buffalo Trace received a Double Gold Rating at the San Francisco World Spirits Competition in 2012. Its distillery has won more awards than any other distillery in the world, with seven 'distillery of the year' titles.

Buffalo Trace

NOSE

Spicy, sweet, caramel, toffee, cinnamon, rum and with cereal sweetness.

TASTE

Brown sugar, apples, toffee, oak, custard, oily, coffee, raisins, chocolate and wood.

APPEARANCE

Pale gold.

JOHNNY DRUM

ABOUT

HISTORY

Johnny Drum is a Kentucky Straight Bourbon whisky, a brand from the Kentucky Bourbon Distillers. Produced in the heart of Kentucky's Bourbon country, Bluegrass, this handmade whisky is made in limited quantities to ensure the highest quality with every bottle. Only the finest natural ingredients are used by this family-run business, whose method of production had remained unchanged throughout five generations to guarantee that the flavour of this rare whisky never changes.

THE BOURBON DISTILLERS

The Kentucky Bourbon Distillers, also known as Willett Distilling Company, are based on the outskirts of Bardstown, Kentucky. It is a privately-owned company, founded by the Willett family who have run the business since it officially opened in 1935, under the Willett company name. Although relatively small, the company is well-known for its dedication to bourbon, as most of its produce is recognised at premium standard. Kentucky Bourbon Distillers hasn't actually acted as a distillery since 1980, therefore most of its bottlings do not distinguish whereabouts they were distilled, and many even retail under fictitious names! However, the company headquarters has recently been refurbished and has been testing a distillation process since 2012, with plans to support pot still and column still distillation equipment.

Johnny Drum

NOSE

Pine trees, campfire smoke, particularly malty when water is added.

TASTE

Smoky, musty, hints of orange and pecans, with a peppery, spicy finish. Hints of mint.

APPEARANCE

Mahogany.

WOODFORD RESERVE

HISTORY

Woodford Reserve is a brand of high-quality Kentucky straight bourbon whisky, which is produced in small batches. Each bottle is numbered with a batch number and bottle number. It's made at the Woodford Reserve Distillery, which is owned by the Brown-Forman Corporation. It's located in Woodford County, central Kentucky.

It was founded by Elijah Pepper and passed on to his son, becoming known as the Oscar Pepper Distillery. The Pepper family sold the distillery to Leopold Labrot and James Graham in 1878, before it was sold again to the Brown-Forman Corporation 63 years later. They kept in in operation for seven years, but then closed it in 1968, selling it on just three years later. Brown-Forman re-purchased the distillery in 1993 and brought it back into full operation. The Woodford Reserve brand became available from 1996.

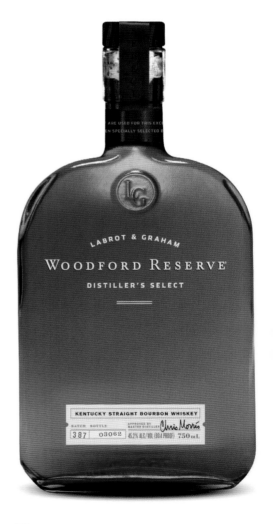

Woodford Reserve

NOSE

Rye, vanilla, cigars with a hint of charcoal and oak.

TASTE

Floral, almonds, marzipan, cocoa and quite dry.

APPEARANCE

Rich amber.

HEAVEN HILL

ABOUT

HISTORY

Heaven Hill was founded shortly after the end of American Prohibition in 1935 by several investors, including prominent distiller, Joseph L. Beam and a member of the Shapira family. It was named after William Heavenhill. Five Shapira brothers – David, Ed, George, Mose and Gary - eventually bought out the other investors. The business began with just 12 employees. The first barrel was filled on 13th December 1935. In 1957 Heaven Hill distilleries launched 'Evan Williams', a bourbon named for the man credited as Kentucky's first distiller. Beam, however, remained as master distiller, with his youngest son, Harry taking over. All master distillers at Heaven Hill have been Beams, and Shapira descendants run the business to this day. Heaven Hill distilleries is America's largest, independent and family-operated producer of distilled spirits.

FIRE

In 1986 Heaven Hill Distilleries launched a small batch bourbon called 'Elijah Craig.' It was named after the so-called 'father of bourbon', a Virginian reverent whose barn caught fire and whose barrels were therefore burnt. Rather than being defeated by this set-back, however, Craig used the barrels to age new whisky and found it improved the colour and flavour. Ironically, ten years later almost all of Heaven Hill's production plant was destroyed by fire. Several warehouses collapsed and more than 90,000 gallons of alcohol were lost.

Heaven Hill

NOSE

Light wood, grains and a hint of charcoal.

TASTE

Maple, dry and tangy.

APPEARANCE

Rich, rusty red.

CANADA

Canadian whisky is made in Canada, usually from rye, and is often referred to as 'rye whisky' as well as 'Canadian whisky'. Rye whisky can in fact be produced anywhere in the world.

ILLICIT EXPORT TO THE UNITED STATES DURING PROHIBITION

Canadian whisky was illegally transported into America during the years of Prohibition. 'Rum-running' or 'bootlegging' as it's called is when alcohol is smuggled into another country either over water or over land. Canadian whisky, like French champagne and English gin, was smuggled into major cities like New York and Boston, where it fetched high prices.

CAPTAIN MCCOY AND CANADIAN WHISKY

With the start of Prohibition, Captain Bill McCoy began to smuggle alcohol into the United States. At one time he had three ships running Irish and Canadian whisky into ports from Maine to Florida. Unlike other captains operating a similar illegal trade, McCoy became famous for never watering down his liquor, only selling top quality brands – hence the phrase 'the real McCoy', meaning something genuine.

HISTORY

The first distillery was established in 1769 in Quebec City. By the 1840s over 200 distilleries were in operation and Canada was earning a reputation as a producer of high quality whisky. Most Canadian whiskies are blended multi-grain liquors, which contain a large amount of corn spirits. Typically they are lighter and smoother than other whisky styles. Canadian whisky often has a distinctive rye-flavoured taste, since it's made primarily from rye and corn, aged in oak barrels for a minimum of three yearS. Canadian whisky accounts for one quarter of the Canadian spirits' market.

IS RYE WHISKY THE SAME AS CANADIAN WHISKY?

Although rye whisky (whisky made from a majority of rye) can be made anywhere in the world – and is, including in America – the terms 'Canadian whisky' and 'rye' have become almost interchangeable in popular thinking. Several hundred years ago Canadian distillers started adding rye grain to their mashes, hence the connection.

However Canadian whiskies are not just made from rye. Whisky products of all types are referred to as 'rye content' and to date there is no labelling dictated by law (as there is in other jurisdictions). In fact, the primary grain used to make most Canadian whisky is corn, which is blended with rye grain after distillation. Canadian law only dictates that all spirits in a Canadian whisky must be aged for at least three years.

Another way that Canadian distillers differ from their counterparts worldwide is that they do no use mash bills (blending grains before fermentation), but instead distill individual grains separately and blend them after distillation or maturation.

CENTENNIAL RYE

ABOUT

HISTORY

Centennial Rye is a Canadian whisky. It is different from other whiskies, since it uses Canadian soft winter wheat in its mash bill with rye grain, rather than corn. This gives it a smooth and rich character. As well as a Centennial Rye ten year old, there is also a Centennial Rye with honey. The ten year old whisky is aged for ten years in chilled and charred oak casks. Highwood distillers produce both whiskies. Highwood distillers was founded in 1974 in High River, Alberta. The distillers bought Potters in 2005 and are now the largest independently owned distillery in Alberta.

RYE: THE POOR COUSIN?

Rye whisky has traditionally been considered inferior to other types of whisky, for example Scottish single malt whiskies. Rye imparts oiliness to a whisky, although many Canadian rye whiskies are made predominantly from corn with barley and wheat in their batches, too.

WHEAT FROM THE PRAIRIES

Centennial Rye is unique in that it's made using grains grown exclusively on the Canadian prairies, before being distilled in Alberta and aged under the Western Canadian climate for a minimum of ten years.

Centennial Rye

NOSE

Grainy, light, fruity and spicy, slight earthiness.

TASTE

Honey, brown sugar, plums, cherries, slightly oily with a hint of molasses and vanilla.

APPEARANCE

Amber.

ABOUT

HISTORY

Seagrams VO is a blended Canadian whisky. In 1913 Joseph E Seagram was working on a very special project in his Ontario Distillery – he wanted to create a special whisky to celebrate his son's wedding. Seagram's VO was the result.

Seagram's Distillery was closed in 1992, but Seagram's VO continues to be produced by multinational Diageo at their distillery in Valleyfield, Quebec with some components for the blend coming from other distilleries.

VO?

The definitive meaning of the letters 'VO' on a bottle of Seagrams is unclear. Some claim 'VO' stands for 'Very Own', referring to the fact that Joseph E. Seagram created the blend for the occasion of his son's wedding. Others claim that 'VO' stands for 'Very Old.' Whatever the truth, perhaps American distiller, Samuel M. Harry, writing about whisky in 1809, was right when he said there were as many myths as truths, when it came to the history of whisky.

HEAD-BANGING LIQUOR

Seagram's VO was the drink of choice for controversial rock star, Alice Cooper, who was dubbed 'the Godfather of Shock Rock' for his unpredictable stage shows. A bottle of Seagrams VO even appeared on the cover of his band's album 'Lace and Whisky' in 1977.

Seagrams VO
Canadian Whisky

NOSE

Rye, earthiness, floral, hint of cream sherry, woody notes and dry grass.

TASTE

Pepper, rye, earthiness, cardamom, nutmeg, ginger, hints of caramel, vanilla and a slight zestiness.

APPEARANCE

Light amber.

POTTER'S

HISTORY

Potter's Special Old Rye Whisky was originally produced by Potter's Distilleries, which was founded by Ernie Potter in 1958.

In 1962 Captain Harold John Cameron Terry – who started his career as an Australian sailor aged just 14 – acquired Potter's Distilleries. In 1990 production was moved from Langley to Kelowna, British Columbia. Then in November 2005 Highwood Distillers purchased Potter's Distilleries, and expanded their portfolio with over a dozen already-established brands, including Potter's whisky itself. Highwood bought all the whisky stocks from the Potter's warehouse in Kelowna, British Colombia to their new warehouse in High River, Alberta, when they bought Potter's Distilleries. There, they continued to let them age. From these stocks, Highwood managed to keep Potter's Whisky brands alive.

Potter's Special Old Rye Whisky is a corn-based whisky, which has been aged in charred American white oak barrels for four to five years. Aged rye grain whisky is added to the blend.

Potter's Special Old Rye Whisky

NOSE

Oily and sweet.

TASTE

Light caramel and very smooth.

APPEARANCE

Light copper.

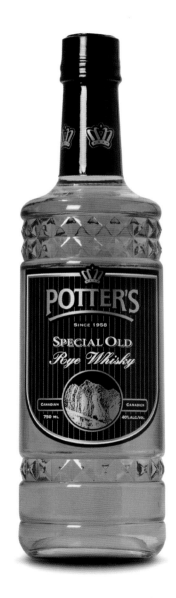

CENTURY RESERVE

ABOUT

HISTORY

Century Reserve is produced by Highwood Distillers in High River, Alberta, Canada. Highwood Distillers is one of Canada's few privately owned distillers. It is a 100% aged corn whisky, with connections to Potter's Distillery, which Highwood bought in 2005 along with all the ageing whisky there.

When Highwood Distillers bought Potter's, they inherited all the whisky stocks dating back to Potter's founding in 1958. Included in the stock was an assortment of casks dating from 15-25 years old. The Century Reserve 15 Years Plus (or Lot 1525) is the bottling of these casks. It's sometimes called Lot 1525, because that is what's stamped on the barrels themselves.

EVERYTHING DONE BY HAND

For the Century Reserve line, everything is done by hand, except for cleaning and filling the bottles. Labels are numbered one by one and applied by hand to each bottle. Fans of Century Reserve often remark upon its distinctive bottle, which has a classic, elegant high neck and gold lettering, both of which imply a high quality product.

Century Reserve Lot 1525

NOSE

Sweet, light and floral.

TASTE

Citrus, oranges, sugary, sweet maple and a touch of vanilla.

APPEARANCE

Pale straw.

STILL WATERS

ABOUT

HISTORY

Still Waters Distillery is a young distillery, having launched in 2009 as the first micro-distillery in Ontario, Canada. Owners and founders Barry Bernstein and Barry Stein pride themselves on their handmade products; all spirits are made in small batches, then bottled and packaged by hand. Still Waters have only just released their first batches of whisky, since Canadian law requires a minimum maturation period of three years. Until recently, the pair had been producing premium-quality vodka, until their whisky was ready to be bottled. Still Waters still retails its award-winning vodka, but their whisky ambitions are now becoming a realisation as they contend with the high demand for Canadian-made whisky outside of Ontario.

HOME GROWN

Still Waters use only Ontario-grown grains for its spirits, and great care goes into the selection of ingredients and the distillation process. The owners believe that although their alcohol production is limited, their 'micro' distillery allows each and every batch to retain a personal touch. The two Barry's oversee the production of every batch to ensure a high quality spirit every time.

Still Water 1+11 Special Blend

NOSE

Rye, linseed oil, and flowers with sweetness, hints of toffee, and citrusy notes.

TASTE

Spice, peppers, sweet caramel with ginger, citrus and oak. A nutty, dry and peppery finish.

APPEARANCE

Dark amber, copper.

WHITE OWL

ABOUT

HISTORY

White Owl Whisky is produced by Highwood Distillers, a well-established Canadian whisky distillery based near the foothills of the Rocky Mountains in Alberta, Canada. White Owl is a blend of several well-aged whiskies, including some that are more than ten years old. By regulation, Canadian whisky must be aged for more than three years. White Owl is the only white Canadian whisky on the market and the only white whisky that has been aged enough to qualify as Canadian whisky. Ingenious because of its colour (or lack of it), White Owl took first prize in the Canadian Whisky Innovations category at the annual Canadian Whisky awards in 2012.

WHITE BY NAME,
WHITE BY NATURE

Usually whiskies take on the colour and taste of the casks they are aged in – resulting in tones ranging from light amber to dark brown. Highwood Distillers filters the whisky through charcoal to remove the colour. White Owl is popular also as a clear, whisky-based mixer and demand for it in Canada is currently high.

White Owl

NOSE

Cream soda, citrus, lemons and limes, fruity, melons, smokey, sweet and a hint of anise.

TASTE

Cherries, strawberries, spices, minty, fresh and a touch of oak.

APPEARANCE

Similar to vodka, clear.

CANADIAN CLUB

CANADA

HISTORY

Canadian Club, popularly known as 'C.C' was first produced in 1858. Hiram Walker was an American grocer and distiller. In 1858 he established a distillery on land in Ontario and began selling his whisky as 'Hiram Walker's Club Whiskey.' It became very popular – a fact which annoyed American distillers, who forced the government to pass a law saying that all foreign whiskies should state their country of origin on the label. In the wake of the controversy, Hiram Walker's Canadian Club whisky became even more popular!

The Hiram Walker and Sons Distillery remained in the Walker family until 1926, when it was sold to Harry C Hatch. Canadian Club whisky is still produced at the distillery site Walker founded. It's now owned by Pernod Ricard and the Canadian Club Brand is owned by Beam Inc.

CLUB WHISKY

Walker's whisky was very popular in the late 1800s in the gentlemen's clubs of America and Canada. For that reason it earned the name 'Club Whisky.' Walker aged his whisky in oak barrels for a minimum of five years. This was unusual at the time.

Canadian Club

NOSE

Barley sugar, aniseed, grass, fennel and straw.

TASTE

Spicy, dark sugars and a hint of rum.

APPEARANCE

Bright gold.

CROWN ROYAL

ABOUT

ROYAL VISIT

British monarch, King George VI and his wife, Queen Elizabeth, visited Canada in 1939. To commemorate the royal visit, Samuel Bronfman, President of the Seagram Company, created Crown Royal whisky, a blended Canadian whisky.

Today Crown Royal is produced at the Crown Royal Distillery, Gimli, on the shores of Lake Winnipeg. Daily production of Crown Royal requires over three million litres of water. The whisky produced at the distillery is stored in two million barrels, located at 46 warehouses over five acres of land. The whisky is blended and bottled in Amherstburg, Ontario.

SPECIAL VARIATIONS

Crown Royal has several variations. Crown Royal Special Reserve was introduced in 1992. It comes in a velvet-like bag with gold-coloured draw-strings. Crown Royal XR (Extra Rare) is a limited-release special blend, available in numbered bottles. It's made from the last batch of whisky that was distilled at the Waterloo distillery, which burned down in 1993, leaving only a few barrels of whisky behind.

Crown Royal

NOSE

Maple syrup, pine, nutty.

TASTE

Caramel, honey and vanilla, with faint notes of oak. A light, balanced finish.

APPEARANCE

Amber, maple, golden.

HISTORY

By the 1840s European settlers had begun to arrive in the region. The town of Collingwood, on Georgian Bay, grew and prospered. In 1967 the Canadian Mist Distillery was built to take advantage of the abundant water supply. Canadian Mist is a blended Canadian whisky produced by the Brown-Forman Corporation.

ACCOLADES

Canadian Mist won a double gold at the 2009 San Francisco World Spirits Competition, which uses blind tastings and expert panels to deliver verdicts on whiskies from all over the world. The San Francisco World Spirits Competition assesses hundreds of entrants every year (over one thousand from at least sixty countries). Unanimous gold votes earn the entrant 'double gold.' Canadian Mist is in the top 10 highest rated Canadian whiskies.

Canadian Mist sources it water from the Georgian Bay – not only one of the largest sources of freshwater in the world, but also one of the freshest. The lake was formed during the last ice age, by glaciers that created and filled a hollow out from the granite rock.

Canadian Mist

NOSE

Light and clean with hints of vanilla and chocolate, plus fudge and polenta.

TASTE

Vanilla, caramel and dark fruit.

APPEARANCE

Pale amber.

FORTY CREEK

HISTORY

Forty Creek is a blended, small batch Canadian whisky, made with rye, barley and corn. It's made by John K. Hall, a first generation whisky maker. John Hall, a seasoned wine maker for over 20 years, started to make Forty Creek in 1992. The distillery is located in Grimsby, Ontario, between Niagara Falls and Hamilton.

John Hall, Forty Creek's distiller and president, makes his whisky in two small pot stills. The larger still is 5,000 litres and the smaller one is 500 litres (just 132 gallons). Hall malts his own barley and puts his corn whisky into used bourbon barrels. Hall tastes all his own barrels and does his own blending. He also makes his own sherry and port and uses the casks to age his whisky.

PIONEERING

John Hall was named 'Pioneer of the Year' in 2007 for his contribution to new ways of thinking and methods in the world of whisky. He has said he wants to enhance the heritage of Canadian whisky. In the 1800s there were over 200 whisky makers in Canada. Now Hall is the only independent whisky maker in all of Ontario.

Forty Creek Barrel Select

NOSE

Toffee, caramel and new leather.

TASTE

Spicy, fruity, orange peels, toffee, syrup with touches of wood.

APPEARANCE

Medium to dark amber.

JAPAN

Japanese whisky production began around 1870. The first distillery in Japan opened at Yamazaki. Japanese whisky is closer in style to Scotch, than it is to Irish, American or Canadian whisky styles and it also takes the same spelling (without an 'e').

JAPAN

FAMOUS FIGURE IN JAPANESE WHISKY

Two of the most influential figures in Japanese whisky are Shinjiro Torii and Masataka Taketsuru.

Masataka Taketsuru is credited with founding Japan's whisky industry. He was born in 1894 in Takehara to a family that had owned a sake brewery since 1733. Aged 35 years old, he took summer classes in organic chemistry at the University of Glasgow in Scotland. He also worked at a number of Scottish distilleries. In 1920 he married Jessie Roberta 'Rita' Cowan, who was Scottish by birth and hailed from Middlecroft, Kirkintilloch. The couple faced opposition from both their families for the marriage. However, they briefly lived in Campbeltown, the 'Victorian capital of whisky making' and Taketsuru worked at the Hazelburn Distillery, which was in operation between 1825 and 1925. At the time, Hazelburn was the largest distillery in the town, making almost two thousand gallons of whisky annually. Soon after, Taketsuru moved back to Japan.

On his return, he worked at Kotobukiya, where he helped to found a whisky distillery. Kotobukiya was owned by Shinjiro Torii, a wine producer. Taketsuru undertook several trips to Europe to research whisky and wine production.

By 1934 Taketsuru had founded his own distilling company. It was called Dai Nippon Kaju K.K. and was on the northern Japanese island of Hokkaido. The island has coastlines on the Sea of Japan, Sea of Okhotsk and the Pacific Ocean. In addition it has a number of mountains, lakes and volcanic plateaus, as well as coastal plains and natural parks. Masataka believed that this part of Japan was most similar to Scotland. Dai Nippon Kaju K.K. was later renamed Nikka.

Nikka whisky as first sold in October 1940. The Nikka Whisky Distilling Company Ltd now has two whisky distilleries – the original one on Hokkaido island and another in Aoba-ku, Sendai in the Miyagi Prefecture, Northern Honshu. This later distillery was founded in 1969. The company also owns the Ben Nevis distillery in Scotland.

Taketsuru died in 1979 aged 85 and is buried with his Scottish wife in Yoichi.

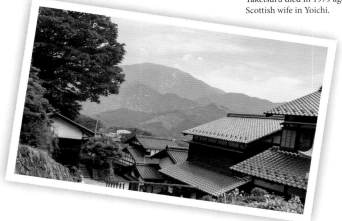

PROHIBITION

Shinjiro Torii was a man who shared Masataka's passion for Japanese whisky. He started importing western liquor and later created 'Akadama Port Wine', which was based on a Portuguese wine recipe. However, his heart was really in the making of Japanese whisky for the Japanese people. Despite opposition from his company's executives, Torii decided to build the first whisky distillery at Yamazaki, a suburb of Kyoto. This area was chosen by legendary tea master, Sen no Rikyu, for the location of his tea-room on the basis of the excellence of its water. Sen Rikyu is considered the most influential historical figure in 'chanoy', the Japanese 'way of tea.' This Japanese tea ceremony involves the ceremonial preparation and presentation of tea. Tea has extremely long, rich and important cultural symbolism for the Japanese.

Having decided on location and build his distillery, Torii invited Taketsuru to be his distillery executive. Torii accepted and brought his knowledge of Scottish whisky making to the first Japanese whisky, helping to establish the Yamazaki Distillery.

NIKKA DISTILLERY

Nikka produces a wide range of Japanese whiskies ranging in quality and price. For example Black Nikka is sold widely in local convenience stores, whereas Nikka Single Cask can fetch up to 15,750 Japanese Yen. In 2008 Yoichi 20 Year Old was voted the best single malt at the World Whisky Awards.

IS JAPANESE WHISKY AS GOOD AS SCOTTISH WHISKY?

For some time it was believed that Japanese whisky could never be as good as its ages-old competitor, Scottish whisky. And for a long time, Japanese whisky only really sold in Japan. However, more recently, blind tastings have put Japanese whisky up there with Scottish whisky for quality and taste – and even, on occasion, scoring higher than their single malt Scottish counterparts.

JAPANESE SINGLE MALTS AND BLENDS

Japanese whisky differs from other whisky production, in that Japanese distilleries are often reluctant to share their whiskies with other distilleries. In other parts of the world, this is not the case and single malts and other varieties of whisky are often sold between distilleries, with each then making its own unique blend. Blended whiskies are by far the biggest types of whisky sold throughout the world. In Japan, therefore, that means that blended whiskies generally only contain malt whisky from the same distillery. Occasionally that's supplemented with exported Scottish whisky. Critics argue that this means there's less raw material for distillers to play with and makes Japanese whisky limited. Fans argue that this limitation means that Japanese distilleries are much more creative and explore a wide range of styles, from light and delicate to heavy and peaty. In 2006 Yoichi was marked with the highest score in 'whisky magazine' in a tasting of 47 brands from around the world by 62 separate judges. Quality comes to Japan!

NIKKA

HISTORY

The Nikka Distilling Company was founded by the 'father of Japanese whisky', Masataka Taketsuru. Taketsuru had travelled to Scotland in the early 1900s to study science and the production of whisky. On his return to Japan, he had one aim: to create quality Japanese whisky and to make the Japanese people fall in love with it. In 1934 Taketsuru established Nikka whisky and built its first distiller in Yoichi, Hokkaido. Nikka now has two malt whisky distilleries – one at Yoichi and the other at Miyagikyo. Nikka produces a range of single malts, single cask whiskies and blends and has won several awards.

SCOTTISH LANDSCAPES

Taketsuru chose both of the locations for his two distilleries based on their similarities to the Scottish whisky-making landscapes that he had known and loved. He believed Hokkaido was most similar to Scotland and therefore the most suitable place to make quality whisky. Yoichi Distillery which is on the same latitude as Toronto in Canada and Vladivostok in Russia, produces a rich and peaty malt. Miyagikyo was selected for whisky production, because of its clean air, humidity and peat-filtered water. It is in northern Japan in Sendai. Taketsuru believed this was the right site for his distillery, as it's enclosed by mountains and has two rivers.

Nikka Whisky

Floral, fruity, spicy and a touch of oak.

Spicy, toffee, caramel, vanilla and fruity.

Old gold.

YAMAZAKI

JAPAN

HISTORY

Yamazaki Distillery is located in Shimamoto, Osaka Prefecture and owned by Suntory. It was opened in 1923 and is Japan's first whisky distillery. 7,000 bottles of unblended malt whisky are on display in its 'whisky library.'

Yamazki was built by one of the founding fathers of the Japanese whisky-making industry – Shinjiro Torii. The distillery is located on the edge of Japan's ancient capital of Kyoto and was chosen for the purity of its water, which had long been praised. Torii also believed that the diversity of climate and high humidity would help his whisky production. Almost a hundred years later, Yamazaki is the most popular single malt whiskies in Japan and is exported to more than 24 countries, including America.

FACING OPPOSITION

Torii introduced whisky to Japan at a time when western culture had not yet pervaded the Land of the Rising Sun. His efforts to make western liquor appealing were initially met with doubts and opposition. In response, he is reported to have said: 'You will never know if your work will end in triumph or mediocrity unless you try.'

Yamazaki 12 Year Old

NOSE

Floral with tropical fruits, nut oils and zesty.

TASTE

Sweet and spicy, with citrus notes, tropical fruit and rum.

APPEARANCE

Golden amber.

HIBIKI

ABOUT

HISTORY

Hibiki is a blended Japanese whisky, which was launched in 1989 to commemorate the 90th anniversary of parent company, Suntory. Suntory was established by Shinjiro Torii, one of the giants in Japanese whisky making. Torii first started the Torii Shoten store in Osaka in 1899.

Some years later, Torii tasted some stored alcohol which he had forgotten about in his shop. He was amazed at the difference in taste and realised that this was what maturation was all about. Soon he became fascinated by the subject and set up the first Japanese whisky distillery. In 1923 Torii completed construction of the Yamazaki distillery, Japans' first malt whisky distillery, located in a tranquil spot near to Kyoto. Hibiki comes from single malts made at the distillery.

MEANING

Hibiki is a Japanese word which can be translated as 'echo' or 'resonance.' One of the malts used in the blends is aged in a Mizunara cask – Mizunara is a rare type of Japanese oak.

Hibiki 12 year old

NOSE

Plum, raspberry, pineapple, honey, raisin and vanilla.

TASTE

Oak, ginger, barley, spices, honey and oaky tones.

APPEARANCE

Amber.

ABOUT

HISTORY

Yoichi is a single malt whisky made by Nikka Whisky Distilling Company in Japan. It takes its name from the Yoichi distillery, which was the first distillery to be set up by founding father of Japanese whisky, Masataka Taketsuru in 1934.

Taketsuru set up his first whisky distillery on the island of Hokkaido, which he believed had a similar climate and landscape to Scotland and was therefore ideally suited for whisky production.

THE YOICHI DISTILLERY

The Yoichi Distillery is located 50km west of Sapporo on the island of Hokkaido in Northern Japan. It has an underground water source that is filtered through peat – ideal for whisky-making. It also has its own kiln, topped with traditional pagoda-shaped chimneys. The pot stills at the distillery are still heated by fire, the traditional method of heating. Situated just one mile from the sea, Yoichi is said also to have a salty tang to it, not dissimilar to coastal Scottish whiskies. Yoichi distillery is built in the same style as traditional Scottish distilleries. It even has its own cooperage and barrels for ageing the spirit are made on site, using new oak.

Yoichi 10 year old

NOSE

Honey, fruity, floral, spicy and with cinnamon.

TASTE

Delicate and smoky, fruity with honey.

APPEARANCE

Pale gold.

ABOUT

HISTORY

The Hakushu Distillery is part of the Suntory group. When Suntory needed a new distillery to meet growing demand for Japanese whisky after World War II, they built the new Hakushu Distillery. At the time, Suntory needed another facility to help their existing distillery at Yamazaki.

HAKUSHU HEIGHTS

Hakushu is the highest distillery in Japan. It is more than two thousand (700 metres) above sea level. The name 'Hakushu' means 'white sand bank'. This is believed to refer to the white sand and stones that can be found in the local streams and rivers. The distillery itself can be found in the middle of forest at the foothills of Mount Kai-Komagatake. Water comes from springs that arise under the foundation of the mountain. Currently there is only one single malt – the 12 year old.

Hakushu Single Malt

NOSE

Light, crisp, hay, sweet mixed peels, nuts and barley malt.

TASTE

Fruits, barley malt, smoky, floral and citrus zest with some spiciness.

APPEARANCE

Light gold.

CHICHIBU

ABOUT

HISTORY

Chichibu is a Japanese single malt whisky. It is produced by Ichiro Akuto's Chichibu Distillery and is aged for three years. Chichibu Distillery is in the hills of the Saitama Prefecture. The distillery began producing Ichiro's malt whisky in 2008. Many have won awards at world competitions and rare bottles from the distillery can fetch high prices among collectors and fans.

WINNING HAND

While setting up the new Chichibu Distillery, Akuto also bottled the Hanyu whisky in limited batches. He chose a playing card to market each release. Collectors snapped up the bottles.

BARLEY FROM EUROPE

Most of the barley currently used is shipped from England, Scotland and Germany, but the distillery has plans to use local barley in the future.

Chichibu

NOSE

Sandalwood with butter and vanilla.

TASTE

Nutty and oily with oak and vanilla.

APPEARANCE

Pale gold.

EUROPE

There are currently over 20 countries, outside the big whisky-producing countries of Scotland, Ireland, the USA and Japan that are distilling single malt whiskies.

EUROPE

EXCITING AND INNOVATIVE NEW EXPERIMENTS

One great advantage European distillers potentially have – and one they are currently exploring – is the availability of barrels which have been pre-used for other alcoholic production, whether that's for Pinot Grigio in Switzerland or Cognac in France. Using barrels in this way could potentially lead to some exciting new tastes in the future.

In relative terms to Ireland and Scotland, for example, whisky production in Europe is at a fairly early stage with new distilleries being set up even now. First bottles from these distilleries cannot be expected to come to market for at least three to ten years. Setting up a distillery is also an expensive process.

NIBBLING AT THE WORLD MARKET

Despite the initial prohibitive set-up costs and long production process, several European distilleries are beginning to make their presence felt on the international stage. Mackymyra is a Swedish distillery, which despite stiff competition from distilleries in Belgium, Holland, France, Wales and England, picked up four medals and a 'European Distiller of the Year' award in 2012.

However, because the European whisky landscape is so young, it is difficult for it to compete with the larger, more established brands from Scotland or Ireland. Give it a few years, however, and experts reckon some European whiskies could be serious competitors for the crown for best world whisky.

EUROPEAN WHISKY DISTILLERS

Europe remains a young, developing market for whisky production, with new distilleries being set up and older, established alcohol producers turning their sights to whisky production. These are the current established European distillers – but there are sure to be more to come.

THE NETHERLANDS

The Netherlands have only been producing whisky for a very short amount of time, with Dutch Jenever proving to be a more popular drink. Gin evolved from Jenever, even though Jenever is very closely related to whisky.

NETHERLANDS

HISTORY OF DUTCH WHISKY

Dutch Jenever is closely related to whisky and Jenever is a more popular just drink. It's unsurprising, therefore, that few whiskies are marketed in the Netherlands, which is more famous for its Jenevers and liqueurs. There are strict EU guidelines governing Jenever production – but, in contrast, nothing nearly as specific for Dutch whisky production.

DOMINANCE OF JENEVER

Jenever (or Genever) is the juniper-flavoured and very alcoholic liquor traditionally popular in the Netherlands and Belgium. Gin evolved from Jenever. There are strict European Union rules specifying that Jenever can only come from the Netherlands, Belgium, two French provinces and two German federal states. It was first sold as a medicine in the late 1500s. Jenever was originally produced by distilling malt wine. Some varieties are still distilled from grain and malt. It is also often matured for a few years in an oak cask. Thus it is very similar in production to whisky, which may be one reason it has retained dominance over whisky production in the Netherlands.

However, two Dutch distilleries are challenging the dominance of Jenever. They are Zuidam and Us Heit.

ZUIDAM

HISTORY

By far and away the biggest distillery in Holland is Zuidam. Zuidam Distillery sits on the Holland-Belgium border and it makes in total over 600 different spirits products. It's been in business since 1975 and is a family-owned company.

In fact, Holland's first whisky was distilled in 1998 at the Zuidam Distillery, although the first Dutch whisky to be bottled was Frysk Hynder from the US Heit Distillery in Bolsward in 2007.

Patrick Zuidam is the current Managing Director. Zuidam was set up by Patrick's father, Fred and his mother, Helene is still involved in its design and packaging. Gilbert, Patrick's brother, is in charge of sales.

Zuidam makes peated and unpeated malt whisky in virgin American oak casks as well as smaller sherry casks. Its range also carries a rye whisky, which is made in small batches. Zuidam's single malt whisky is called Millstone. The first batches were made in 1997 and it is just now coming to market. It's available in four countries currently – the Netherlands, Belgium, Denmark and Japan. Local windmills produce the barley, which goes into this single malt. It is double distilled in hand-made copper pot stills.

Millstone

NOSE

Citrus fruit and spicy with delicate tones of honey, vanilla and oak.

TASTE

Sweet and fruity with tones of honey, delicate spicy notes with a peppery, vanilla and oak finish.

APPEARANCE

Dark toffee gold.

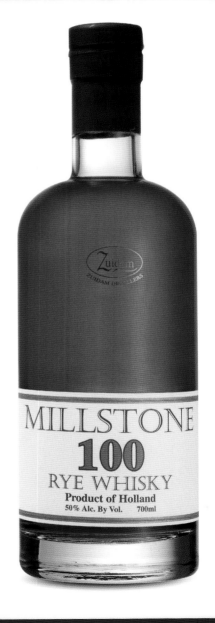

ENGLAND

There are currently three distilleries producing whisky in England. Whisky-producing giants and neighbours, Ireland and Scotland, have always traditionally overshadowed England. Although England is not famous for producing whisky, until the later 1800s there were distillers operating in London, Liverpool and Bristol.

ENGLAND

HISTORY

In his reference book 'The Whisky Distilleries of the United Kingdom' of 1887 Alfred Barnard listed four English distilleries. They were –

- Lea Valley Distillery in Stratford, East London. Lea Valley was founded in the late 1800s and produced both malt and grain whisky.

- Bank Hall Distillery in Liverpool, which produced both malt and grain whisky.

- Bristol Distillery, which was founded in the 1600s in the city of its name and produced grain whisky, which was sent to Scotland and Ireland for blending.

- Vauxhall Distillery in Liverpool, which was founded in 1781 and produced grain whisky.

Production of English single malt whisky ended around 1905, when the Lea Valley Distillery closed.

CORNISH REVIVAL

After this date, production of English single malt whisky did not occur again until 2003, when the St Austell brewery and Healey Cyder Farm announced the first production of a Cornish single malt whisky for 300 years. It was the first commercial whisky to be produced in England in over a century. St Austell Brewery and Healey Cyder Farm also released a seven-year-old whisky in 2011, opting for the 'whiskey' variation in spelling. That aside, critics hailed this debut whisky as one of the finest they'd tasted. Some proceeds from the sale of the whisky went to local charities.

THE ENGLISH WHISKY CO.

ENGLAND

HISTORY

This Cornish whisky is made with barley grown in southeast Cornwall, the wash is fermented at St Austell Brewery's Victorian brew-house and it is then transported to Healey Cyder Farm. The wash is double distilled in copper pot stills and aged in American bourbon charred oak casks.

THE ENGLISH WHISKY CO.

The English Whisky Co. was founded by farmer James Nelstrop and is based in Roundham, Norfolk – as far east as St Austell Brewery and Healey's Cornish Cyder Farm is west! St George's Distillery began production in 2006.

It produces single malt whisky and its first whisky, three years old, came onto the market in 2009. The grain for the whisky comes from nearby Fakenham, the yeast from Kingston-Upon-Hull in neighbouring county, Lincolnshire, and the water comes from Breckland, an unusual gorse-covered sand heath that covers part of southern Norfolk. Nelstrop said it was the fulfilment of a 45-year-old dream to make whisky in Norfolk, saying that barley has traditionally been sent from Norfolk to Scotland to make whisky. St George's distillery has released a range of aged malt spirits and single malt whiskies.

English Single Malt Whisky

NOSE

Barley, grassy, vanilla, lime, bananas and pears with a touch of caramel and marzipan.

TASTE

Oaky, caramel, toasted grains, apricots, fudge, nutty and a touch of lemon.

APPEARANCE

Pale yellow, like chardonnay wine.

FRANCE

FRANCE

Famed more for its liqueurs, wines and Champagnes, France has never been a big whisky producer. But France does have one big advantage when it comes to whisky production – readily available barrels from its world-renowned wine production. Different barrels produce different tastes and French distillers are beginning to take advantage of what's already on their doorstep. Not only that, but a long tradition making other spirits, such as brandy, means there's distillation expertise in France with the necessary equipment to make whisky.

OLD DOG, NEW TRICKS

Wambrechies Distillery, in Northern France, started out as a gin Distillery in 1817. Nowadays it makes single malt whisky. Warenghem Distillery, in Brittany, founded in 1900 by Leon Warenghem, also started off making cider and fruit spirits. Since 1987 it, too, has been producing whisky. Another old distillery, Bertrand Distillery, which was formed in 1874, has been producing whisky since 2002. It uses malt sourced locally. Barrels come from Alsace, home of the distillery.

Daucourt Distillery is owned by Jean-Marc Daucourt. Daucourt previously worked at a Scottish whisky distillery, before travelling the world to learn more about the art of distillation. Returning home with a vision to produce French whisky, he founded Daucourt Distillery, which began to offer 'Bastille 1789 Hand-Crafted Whisky' in the States in 2012. Bastille 1789 whisky is made from barley and wheat grown in north-east France. Water comes from the Gensac Spring, filtering through the limestone of the Grande Champagne district of Cognac in southwestern France.

RELATIVE NEWCOMERS

Guillon Distillery in Louvois was founded in 1997 by Thierry Guillon. It started distilling whisky two years later. Guillon Distillery age their whiskies in barrels previously used for white, red and fortified wine maturation - quite often sweet wines - which give their whiskies a unique taste.

Another relative newcomer to the world of whisky is Des Menhirs Distillery in Brittany. Although founded in 1986, it didn't start producing whisky until 1998. Des Menhirs produces 'Eddu', a Breton word for buckwheat - which is one of the ingredients of their whisky.

Glann ar Mor is another Breton distillery – the name means 'by the sea'. It was founded in 1999 and began whisky production in 2005. It released its first malt in 2008.

Two French companies based on the island of Corsica – Domaine Mavel and Brasserie Pietra – have also come together to form a whisky-producing partnership, known as P&M. Pietra produces mash that is distilled at the Mavela distillery.

BRENNE

ABOUT

HISTORY

Brenne is a French single malt whisky. Brenne was launched on the 1st October 2012 to a market in New York, USA. Since that time its market has been expanding. Each bottle of Brenne comes from a single barrel and the barrel number is stamped on the bottle's label. Since the spirit is selected at what is considered its optimum time, the ageing of each batch differs, although on average it's aged for about seven years.

FOUNDED BY A WOMAN

Allison Patel founded Brenne. Patel had a passion to introduce lesser-known whiskies to the US market, particularly those that were handcrafted. Her dream was born out a passion for food and drink, which she shares with her husband, Nital. When Nital kept discovering whiskies from around the world that were unavailable in the US, the couple decided they wanted to change the situation. Patel began to explore the world of handcrafted whisky. When she met a third generation Cognac distiller, she knew she'd found the expertise to help create a single malt whisky out of the heart of France.

FRENCH PEDIGREE

Brenne is made from 100% organic ingredients. It is distilled at the Brenne Estate in the Cognac region of France using organic malted barley and pure water from the Charente region. Brenne is double-distilled in copper Alembic stills and then matured in French Limousin oak barrels for a minimum of six years. After that, the spirit is transferred to Cognac casks for further maturation.

French Single Malt Whisky

NOSE

Almond, vanilla, apricot, apple and hints of dark chocolate.

TASTE

Chocolate, orange peel, butter, warm spices and a touch of peppercorns and cloves.

APPEARANCE

Light golden.

SWEDEN

The Swedish whisky-making industry is young. Swedish entry into the European Union paved the way for privately-owned distilleries in Sweden. Before this time, strict Swedish alcohol legislation did not allow such enterprises. That's not to say that Swedes don't drink whisky – they do – but everything until recently had to be imported.

During the last decade, several whisky companies have started in Sweden. They are now at different stages of their growth, from choosing locations to bringing products to market.

SWEDEN

Currently, the Mackmyra Distillery is the only distillery that has its own whisky on the market. They have now released many whiskies of different styles all of which have been well received, and not only in Sweden. Other distilleries that are expected to release their own whiskies include the Adalen Distillery, the Gammelstilla Distillery and the Grythyttan Distillery.

The smallest whisky distillery in Sweden is called Smogen Whisky, with an expected production of just 5000 litres in six months. Smogen intends to produce a highly peated whisky, using imported malted barley from Scotland. The company is run by whisky enthusiast and publisher writer Per Caldenby.

MACKMYRA

HISTORY

Mackmyra Whisky is a Swedish whisky distillery and is currently the only one that has brought products to market. Eight classmates from the Royal Institute of Technology in Stockholm founded it in 1999. It's located at the old Mackmyra Bruk (power plant) facilities in the village of Mackmyra in central Sweden.

While the founders were trying to test their ideas, they tried more than 150 different recipes, adjusting the barley used, the smoke fuel and the yeast brands. Products from this time are currently stored in about 50 barrels in a cool warehouse. The barrels range in size from 30 to 100 litres and contain in total around 3,000 litres. Some of the barrels are made from Swedish oak, some are remade bourbon barrels and some are old sherry barrels. The commercial distillery opened near the end of 2002.

The first bottlings from Mackmyra sold out just hours after release. Yearly production is currently at around 200,000 litres – the equivalent of half a million bottles of whisky.

Mackmyra Single Malt Whisky

NOSE

Fruity, citrus, honey, lightly spicy, oaky and with a touch of toffee.

TASTE

Fruity, honey and with spices, including spiced apples.

APPEARANCE

Pale yellow.

WALES

Wales began producing whisky in the Middle Ages, but production of Welsh whisky died out in the 19th Century. Today, there is only one working whisky distillery in the whole country.

WALES

PAST

Whisky has been distilled in Wales since the Middle Ages. The Great Welsh Warrior Reaulty Hir is said to have distilled 'chwisgi' from braggot brewed by the monks of Bardsey Island as early as 356 AD. Braggot was a type of mead or honey wine common in medieval times.

Production of Welsh whisky died out in the late 1800s, probably heavily influenced by the temperance movement. The temperance movement urged a reduced or prohibited consumption of alcohol. The last notable distillery of this time was at Frongoch and had been established by R J Lloyd Price in 1887. His company, the 'welsh

whisky distillery company' was unsuccessful and was sold in 1900 to William Owen of Bala for £5000. Just ten years later it was liquidated.

Welsh whisky production lay dormant for almost the rest of the century, until the 1990s when entrepreneurs attempted to rouse it again. First efforts centred around bottling Scottish blends on Welsh soil and labelling them 'welsh whisky.' A lawsuit by Scottish distillers soon put an end to that, however.

Finally at the turn of the millennium in 2000, a distillery was built at Penderyn in the Brecon Beacons National Park. Four years later, its first product went on sale.

PENDERYN

THE FUTURE

Penderyn is the first whisky that is commercially available and made in Wales since the nineteenth century. It's a single malt whisky and is distilled in the village of Penderyn, from which it gets its name. Penderyn is the only whisky currently produced in Wales.

Penderyn Distillery itself is situated in Brecon Beacons National Park, which is part of a mountain range in South Wales and includes Wales' highest mountain, Pen y Fan. UNESCO has recognised the region's importance. In fact, there are six main peaks in the park and Brecon Beacons itself is said to have been named after the ancient practise of lighting signal fires (beacons) on mountains to warn of attacks by invaders. The area is known for its beauty, its valleys and its waterfalls, as well as its mountains. The famous Sgwd-yr-Eira waterfall is within walking distance of the distillery.

Penderyn brewery obtains its wash from Brains Brewery. It launched its first single malt on St David's day, 1st March, 2004 in the presence of Prince Charles. St David is the patron saint of Wales. In 2008 Prince Charles, Prince of Wales, opened a visitors' centre at Penderyn.

Penderyn remains a small distillery – some premium brand distilleries produce more whisky in a day than Penderyn produces in a year, although Penderyn produces high quality whisky in small batches, just one cask per day. Despite its small output, Penderyn is gaining an international reputation.

Penderyn Single Malt Whisky

NOSE

Intense peachy sweetness, with mango, grape, apples and melon.

TASTE

Spicy, fruity, custard, melon and marmalade.

APPEARANCE

Soft gold.

SWITZERLAND

Switzerland is not well known for its whisky, but it imports almost two million litres a year. In addition, there are almost 60 brands of whisky in Switzerland, which come from about 20 different distillers, who, between them, produce around 55,000 home-grown litres per year. Amazingly, whisky production has only been legal in Switzerland since 1st July, 1999. Until that date, Swiss law prohibited the use of staple foods, such as grains and potatoes, in distilling. Now Swiss law only allows a distillate made from malt to be called whisky after it has aged for at least three years (like Scottish and Canadian whiskies).

SWITZERLA

Switzerland's first whisky was called Holle Single Malt, produced in the 1990s by the Bader family who owned a farm where they distilled their own brandy. They decided to create whisky, which was aged in white and red Burgundy barrels. The largest independent distillery in the country is now the Locher Brewery, who produce Santis Malt whisky. Santis Malt has received many awards, including 'European Whisky of the Year

2010'. Interestingly, many distilleries now producing whisky in Switzerland began by producing traditional fruity brandy.

Swiss law dictates that a malt distillate must be aged for a minimum of three years in order to be called whisky – much like the Scottish law. The Swiss also opted to keep the traditional spelling of 'whisky' (minus the 'e'), as they much admired the traditions of Scotch whisky.

ABOUT

HISTORY

Santis Malt whisky is distilled at the Locher Brewery which is situated in the heart of Appenzell, Switzerland. The Locher family have owned the business for five generations, producing spirits and beers for over 100 years. Despite the brewery's success, it only began to produce whisky in 1999 after the Swiss ban on manufacturing spirits from grain, was lifted. In 2003, the Locher Brewery began to use raw ingredients from the Swiss mountains to enhance the exquisite flavour of their whisky, and to sustain the agriculture of the Swiss mountain area. The extreme weather conditions are said to give the grain a more 'vigorous' flavour, contributing to the quality of the whisky.

UNCONVENTIONAL APPEAL

Santis Malt is matured in historical beer barrels made of oak, and is uniquely made with spring water from the Alpstein Mountains. The first bottles were launched in 2002 after a maturation period of three years, and four different editions were released, each named after a different Alpstein rock formation. Santis Malt was well received, and one expression was named 'European Whisky of the Year 2010'.

Santis Malt

NOSE

Sweet, aromas of apple, and a slight woodiness.

TASTE

Fresh, oaky and fruity, particularly apples. A short but satisfying finish.

APPEARANCE

Gold.

REST OF THE WORLD

There are currently over 20 countries, outside the big whisky-producing countries of Scotland, Ireland, the USA and Japan, that are distilling single malt whiskies.

AFRICAN WHISKY

Premier whisky production centres on South Africa, where whisky is very popular. The James Sedgwick Distillery has existed in South Africa since the late 1800s and started to make whisky in 1990.

In 2013, South Africa's first single grain whisky from the distillery, Bain's Cape Mountain Whisky, was awarded the 'world's best grain whisky' at the prestigious Whisky Magazine's World Whisky Awards, held in London every year. Tastings are done blind, based on three tasting rounds from a panel of international experts. Bain's Cape Mountain whisky beat off competition from well-established whisky-producing countries as Scotland, Ireland and the USA.

Bain's Cape Mountain whisky was launched in 2009 and is made from South African grains, which are fermented and distilled locally. In South Africa the maize used in Bain's Cape Mountain whisky is informally known as 'mealies.'

The previous year, 2012, Three Ships 5 year old, another South African whisky, won 'world's best blended whisky' at the same awards. Although South Africa doesn't have the scale of a whisky-producing giant such as the States or the long and historical reputation of a country like Scotland, these new whiskies are certainly putting Africa firmly on the map in terms of quality and excellence in the world market.

ASIAN WHISKY

Asian whisky is perhaps dominated by whisky-producing Japan, where the spirit has been in production since 1924, when its first distillery, Yamazaki, was opened. Japanese whisky is undoubtedly influenced by Scottish whisky, because of strong connections to Scottish whisky production methods through some of Japanese whiskies founding fathers. Nowadays Japanese whisky is dominated by two distilleries, Suntory and Nikka. Both produce single malt and blended whiskies. In blind tastings, Japanese whisky scores well, often out-classing its more established rivals, such as Scotland.

Indian whisky is another story, however. Much of what passes for whisky in India is, in fact, a liquor made using molasses, in a similar way to rum. There is an on-going debate in the whisky world about whether this constitutes true whisky! Free from this controversy, however, is an Indian single malt called 'Amrut' from Bangalore, which has received positive critical acclaim. Trade tarrifs mean that, for now, Indian 'whisky' remains a popular choice mostly for whisky-loving Indians in what is a large and growing market.

AUSTRALIAN AND NEW ZEALAND WHISKY

At first glance, the climate of Australia – the driest on the planet – wouldn't seem to lend itself to whisky-making - a chief ingredient of which is water. However, the Tasmanian highlands, which are home to clear water, peaty bogs and a cool climate are beginning to produce some New World whiskies of note, particularly single malts. There are over ten distillers or whisky bottlers in Tasmania. New legislation in the region favours small-scale, high quality, hand-crafted whiskies, which are sure to impress global whisky drinkers and gain a positive reputation.

SOUTH AFRICA

Whisky is very popular in South Africa, where a range of styles including single malts are produced. Although it isn't a traditional whisky-producing country, like Ireland or Scotland, South Africa is beginning to gain traction in the world of whisky making.

Partly, perhaps, this is to do with South Africa's warm climate, which helps to accelerate the ageing process, creating whiskies that have a lot of smoothness due to a faster interaction between wood, spirit and air. Higher ambient temperatures (as opposed, for example, to a chilly Scottish climate), may mean whiskies may mature at a younger age.

Two South African whiskies of note currently are Bain's Cape Mountain whisky and Three Ships whisky.

SOUTH AFRICA

THREE SHIPS

ABOUT

In 1886 J Sedgwick and Company Ltd bought a distillery on the banks of the Berg River in Wellington. The aim was to distil brandy. The distillery moved into whisky production. Three Ships Bourbon Cask Finish won gold at the International Wine and Spirit Competition in 2008, 2010 and 2012. In addition, it has won 'Best Rest of the World blended whisky' at the World Whiskies Award and has gained critical acclaim.

GROWTH

Whisky is the fastest growing liquor in South Africa, currently outpacing cider and beer. Top imports into South Africa include Bell's, Johnnie Walter, Firstwatch, Black & White and J&B. Growth is partly attributed to an upswing in demand from middle-class black families, who are switching from brandy to whisky as their drink of choice. As well, Robby's bar in Soweto sells a case of whisky every day.

South Africa is currently the sixth largest global market for whisky, with premium and super-premium whiskies making up almost 90% of sales. The future of whisky consumption is likely to be in Africa, Latin America and Asia.

South Africa's quality, home-grown brands can only grow in popularity.

Three Ships 5 Year Old

NOSE

Creamy fudge, sultanas, faintly peaty.

TASTE

Fudge, subtle smoke, pepper, spicy and oily.

APPEARANCE

Copper.

INDIA

INDIA

The drinking of whisky was introduced into India in the nineteenth century, during the British Raj. The British Raj is the term used for British rule in the Indian subcontinent during 1858-1947.

Scotch-style whisky is the most popular distilled alcoholic drink in India and whisky has become fashionable for wealthier Indians. However, distilled alcoholic drinks labelled as 'whisky' in India are most commonly blends based on neutral spirits that are distilled from fermented molasses with only a small proportion consisting of malt whisky and that in quantities of less than 20%. 90% of all whisky consumed in India currently is molasses-based.

India has the biggest global consumer of whisky at 70 million cases per year, but 99% of whisky sold in India is made locally.

ABOUT

Amrut Distilleries Limited is a part of the N. R Jagdale Group, based in Bangalore, India and was established in 1948. It has produced the first single malt whisky to be made in India – Amrut Single Malt – launched in 2004. Amrut Single Malt has gone on to win a range of awards and critical acclaim. In 2012 Amrut Distileries won 'whisky ambassador of the year' and the 'new world whisky' title. Amrut Single Malt is made from 100% Indian barley, grown in Punjab and Rajasthan, which is then mashed, distilled and aged in Bangalore.

Amrut Fusion Single Malt Whisky

NOSE

Vanilla, cinnamon, almonds and smoky ginger.

TASTE

Fruity, with figs, spices, plain chocolate, peat and a touch of leather and blood orange.

APPEARANCE

Deep amber.

AUSTRALIA

Despite historical links to Ireland and Scotland, Australia has never been a big producer of whisky. The first Australian single malt was made in the late 1990s and is called Sullivan's Cove. Lark Distillery, based in Tasmania, has also been in production since 1992. Australian whiskies are currently increasing and gaining whisky awards and medals with a significant number of distilleries based in Tasmania.

AUSTRALIA

TASMANIAN DEVIL

Tasmania is an island state located 240km off mainland Australia and separated by the Bass Strait. The state has a population of just over half a million. It has a largely unspoiled natural environment, with over 45% of the island lying in reserves, national parks and World Heritage Sites. Its mountainous landscape and lakes with coastal plains and farmland are possibly what make it a popular location for whisky production. It also has a cool temperate climate. In 1824 Hobart had 16 legal distilleries and many more illegal stills. In 1838, however, Governor John Franklin imposed a total prohibition on distilling that lasted 150 years and was only overturned in the early 1990s. Since then Tasmanian distilleries have been growing in number and quality.

UP WITH THE LARKS

Lark Distillery was the first licensed distillery in Tasmania since 1839. It was established in 1992 to produce Australian malt whisky. Lark Distillery is one of Australia's leading distilleries, running a 1800 litre copper pot still that can produce 10-12 one hundred litre barrels per month.

Bill Lark realised that Tasmania had everything needed to make premium whisky – fields of barley, pure water, highland peat bogs and a good climate. Lark's interest in home-grown whisky grew through a conversation he had with his father-in-law. As the two sipped single malt whisky on a fishing trip, Lark wondered why there was no one making malt whisky in Tasmania: Lark Distillery was born. Bill's wife, Kirsty Lark, is master distiller and is one of the world's youngest female distillers.

SULLIVAN'S COVE

ABOUT

Sullivan's Cove has been named best Australian single malt. Sullivan's Cove whisky was established in 1994 in Hobart. It uses only Tasmanian ingredients. It is not chill filtered and has no other flavours or colours added to it. This purist approach means that each barrel is bottled individually to respect the natural differences that occur from barrel to barrel.

Sullivan's Cove
Double Cask Single Malt

NOSE

Vanilla, cocoa, toffee and spices, with a hint of liquorice and pepper.

TASTE

Chocolate, honeycomb and rich plum pudding with soft vanilla.

APPEARANCE

Brilliant gold.

ABOUT

NOWT LIKE NANT

The Nant Distillery is another Tasmanian distillery. The Batt family acquired the estate on which it sits in 2004, restoring an old water-driven flour mill as part of the process. The Mill, which dates from 1823, is now a fully-functioning whisky distillery, producing single malt whisky in small batches. It uses traditional pot still distillation, Tasmanian barley and water sourced from the highland lakes. Tasmanian Highland single malt whisky is the result.

Nant Cask 6 Single Malt

NOSE

Rich and smooth, raisins with Madeira and a hint of liquorice, cinnamon and caramel.

TASTE

Buttery and spicy with raisins, cinnamon, dark chocolate, coffee and liquorice.

APPEARANCE

Old gold.

Picture Credits

Amrut Distilleries 121

Asahi Group Holdings 96, 99

Basis Group 125

Brenne Estate 109

Brown Forman 78, 90

Buffalo Trace Distillery 76

Bushmills Distillery 52

Campari 73

Caroline Icke 25, 26, 28, 31, 32, 33, 35, 37, 38, 39, 40, 42, 43, 44, 45, 47, 53, 55, 56, 59, 60, 61, 69, 72, 74, 77, 83, 88, 89, 97, 98, 100, 101, 113

De Kock Communications 119

DVL Public Relations 70

Edelman 71

Edrington Group 27, 46

Forty Creek Distillery 91

Glen Fahrn 115

Heaven Hill Distillery 79

Highwood Distillers 82, 84, 85, 87

International Beverage 24, 30, 34

Mackmyra Distillery 111

Morrison Bowmore 36, 41

Richmond Towers Communications 29, 54, 57

Sazerac 68, 75

St. George's Distillery 107

Steely Fox 58

Still Waters Distillery 86

Tasmania Distillery 124

Zuidam Distillers 105

With special thanks to The Wee Dram for their help in providing whiskies for use in photographs, and their kind and knowledgeable assistance. The Wee Dram, 5 Portland Square, Bakewell, Derbyshire, DE45 1HA

Index

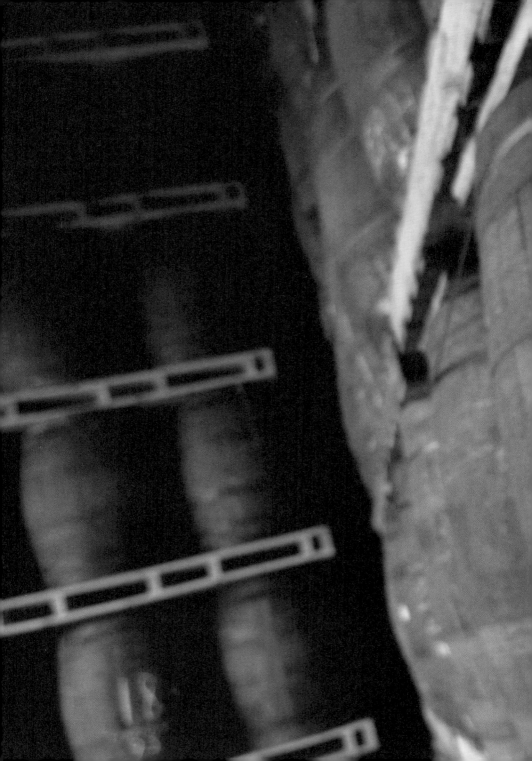